LATIN POETRY

FOR THE BEGINNING STUDENT

LATIN POETRY

FOR THE BEGINNING STUDENT

Student Edition

Edited by

RICHARD A. LaFLEUR

University of Georgia
Athens, Georgia

Contributors

Martha Jones
Richard A. LaFleur
Tyler Lansford
Laurie Lawless
Constance Lederer
Mary Ruth Malone
Wallace B. Ragan
Ilse Stratton

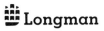 Longman

VXORI CARISSIMAE ET LIBERIS AMATIS

Longman, 10 Bank Street, White Plains, N.Y. 10606

Associated companies:
Longman Group Ltd., London
Longman Cheshire Pty., Melbourne
Longman Paul Pty., Auckland
Copp Clark Pitman, Toronto
Pitman Publishing Inc., New York

ISBN   0-8013-0133-5

7 8 9 10-CRC-999897

CONTENTS

AN INTRODUCTION TO LATIN POETRY

The earliest European works of literature, Homer's *Iliad* and *Odyssey,* were set to meter, both as an aid to memory (Homer's epics were composed and transmitted orally for some generations before finally being written down in the eighth or seventh century B.C.) and to appeal to our innate sense of rhythm. In content this early poetry was narrative, it told a story. In the *Iliad* it was a very human tale of the proud but impulsive Greek hero Achilles, his inept commander Agamemnon, and the Trojan prince Hector, of their complex motives in fighting the Trojan War, and of their courage, their weaknesses, and their suffering; in the *Odyssey* it was the exciting saga of Achilles' fellow warrior, the wily Odysseus (Ulysses, as the Romans called him), and the many perils he encountered and overcame during his return from the war to his homeland of Ithaca and his ever-faithful spouse Penelope. It would be an understatement to say that these poems, still widely read today, were enormously popular among the Greeks and even the Romans, who admired, embraced, and emulated so much of Greek literature and art.

Poetry in general was greatly appreciated by the ancients. Even their stage plays, tragedies and comedies alike, were in verse; and, both in public performance and at private dinner parties, a favorite entertainment was the recitation of poetry, whether epic, romantic, or comic. The reasons for their special attraction to poetry were many and complex, involving in certain instances even politics and religion. But the fundamental explanation, and one that applies equally well to our own love of verse and song today, was understood well enough by the Greek philosopher Aristotle: man is attracted instinctively both to rhythm and to storytelling, or "mimesis," as Aristotle called it, the dramatic representation of human action. We are all mimetic creatures—we love to tell tales, hear them, see them. And we are certainly all by nature creatures of rhythm, the rhythms of the seasons, of night and day, of our heartbeats. We are all, I might add, however well or poorly educated, infinitely susceptible to the power of words artfully arranged and expressively uttered.

The assumption that this phenomenon applies at least as much to the beginning Latin student as it does to others of the human species has provided the stimulus for this little text. However regrettable, it is a fact that the majority of Latin students today, especially those in the high schools, enroll in only one or two courses in the language (*lector cārissime:* be the exception!). Since "real" Latin of any sort, that is, continuous, unadapted passages from ancient authors, is generally not encountered before the second course, and Latin verse rarely before the third or even the fourth, most Latin students miss the opportunity of reading any significant excerpts from the works of some of Rome's most admired and influential authors.

This reader, which is intended for use as a supplement to any first- or second-year Latin text, aims to remedy that situation by presenting in eight units a brief sampling from some of the most popular Latin poetry. The eight units, which are arranged chronologically but which may be read in any order, include two of Catullus' lyric poems to his paramour Lesbia, Dido's suicide scene from Vergil's *Aeneid,* Horace's ode on the death of the Egyptian queen Cleopatra, excerpts from Ovid's accounts of the legend of Romulus and Remus (from his poem entitled the *Fasti*) and of the mythical Golden Age (from the *Metamorphoses*), several of Martial's epigrams describing the dedication of the Colosseum and some of the entertainments produced in that arena, a portion of Juvenal's satiric depiction of the dangers risked in venturing out into the streets of Rome by night, and, finally, the book's one non-classical selection, Thomas of Celano's well-known Christian hymn on the Day of Judgment, the *Dies Irae.* Each unit is prefaced by a brief introduction to the poet's life and works and comments on the particular selection(s) presented, which may be supplemented by your instructor through the assignment of outside readings, class reports, or other activities.

All the Latin is unadapted, that is to say, it has not been altered or "simplified" in any way. As an aid to reading, the Latin text, which appears on the left-hand page, is equipped with vocabulary and other notes on the facing page. Most words that you have likely not yet encountered in your study of Latin are glossed in these notes; others you can either locate in the vocabulary section of your primary Latin textbook or define, as in the case of *clāmor* in Unit Two or *liquidās* in Unit Five, on the basis of English derivatives. Full principal parts are given for verbs, and nominative, genitive, and gender, for nouns. Any constructions and forms that may be unfamiliar, such as subjunctives, participles, gerunds, supines, and deponents, are translated in the notes, which will also call your attention to peculiarities of word order common to poetry (adjectives are often far removed from the nouns they modify, prepositions sometimes follow their objects, conjunctions occasionally appear as the second or third word in a clause, rather than at the beginning). The few abbreviations employed are all standard: M., F., N., and C., for masculine, feminine, neuter, and common gender; sing. and pl. for singular and plural; nom., gen., dat., acc., abl., and voc., for the cases; B.C. and A.D. for before and after Christ; cf., for Latin *cōnfer,* "compare"; ca., for *circā,* "about" or "approximately"; i.e., for *id est,* "that is"; and sc., for *scīlicet,* "understand" or "supply."

Comprehension questions are also included in each unit. Designed to focus attention upon, and test your comprehension of, essential details of the narrative, these are objective, factual questions which may be answered, either in Latin or in English, through direct reference to the text.

Reading Latin Poetry Aloud

As suggested earlier, ancient poetry was composed to be read aloud (or, in certain instances, to be sung or chanted to musical accompaniment) and with the listening audience, not the reading audience, foremost in mind. The Latin poet hoped to appeal at once to the intellect and to the emotions—in varying proportion, depending upon the particular genre—and his approach to both was through the ear. Both the "music" and the "message" of poetry derived in part from its sound effects: its rhythm and assonance and such devices as alliteration and onomatopoeia might contribute much to the overall effect of a poem. When we read silently, therefore, or aloud but unexpressively, we are neglecting altogether an important aspect of the poet's artistry, just as surely as if we were to experience the colorful paintings of Gauguin or Picasso only through the medium of black and white photographs.

Reading poetry or prose aloud in an expressive manner even in our native tongue requires some deliberate effort and practice, as you very well know, and certainly at least as much effort will be necessary to develop your skills in reading Latin orally. But the task is far from Herculean, and is best approached by stages.

1. *Correct Pronunciation*

The first and most important step in any beginning language course is to learn the sounds of the language, that is the correct pronunciation, and to exercise that knowledge through listening and speaking activities every day. Though Latin in its classical form is not spoken today, we do have abundant evidence of how it was spoken by the Romans from ancient testimony (a first-century B.C. Roman named Varro, for example, wrote a detailed monograph *De Lingua Latina,* portions of which have survived), from the way it has developed into its various modern forms (in Italian, French, Spanish, and the other Romance languages), and even from phonologically-based spelling errors found in graffiti and other ancient texts (just as the misspelling "kat" might tell non-English speakers something about one pronunciation of the letter *c*). Very straightforward rules for the pronunciation of classical Latin (some of the differences in medieval Latin are noted below, in the *Dies Irae* unit) are provided in the introduction of every beginning Latin text; again, they should be learned and applied every day in listening and oral reading exercises. The first step in reading a Latin poem aloud, then, is simply to read each sentence from beginning to end, following the rules for classical Latin pronunciation that you have already learned.

2. *Meter*

As you read, and especially if your pronunciation is careful and accurately reflects the differences between long and short vowels, the proper sounds of diphthongs (*ae, oe, ei, ui, au,* and *eu*), and so forth, you may detect a certain rhythmical pattern in the arrangement of the words. This, of course, reflects what Roger Hornsby has called "a vital, indeed a primordial, aspect of poetry," *meter* (from the Latin *metrum* and Greek *metron*, meaning "measure"), which may be defined as the measured arrangement of syllables in a regular rhythmical pattern. In English verse, as you know, and in the very earliest Latin verse, meter is determined by the patterned alternation of accented and unaccented syllables, an accented syllable being one that is spoken with greater stress or emphasis, such as the syllable *mid-*, in "Ońce ūpón ā mídnīght dréarȳ" (which is here "scanned," the "scansion" indicating schematically the accented [´] and unaccented [ˉ] syllables).

In classical Greek, normal word accent was based upon pitch rather than stress (the language was therefore by nature far more "musical" than either Latin or English) and was not the prime determinant in verse rhythm. Rather than being "qualitative" (i.e., based on the stress quality of a syllable), Greek meter was "quantitative" (i.e., based on the quantity, or length, of a syllable); and, though it was not entirely suited to their own stress-accented language, the Romans adapted the use of quantitative meter to their verse from the time of the early epic poet Ennius (239-169 B.C.) onward (there was a return to qualitative meter in Latin verse during the Middle Ages, as is seen in the *Dies Irae* in Unit Eight).

That syllables may be defined in terms of quantity, i.e., that some may be "long" and others "short," is clear enough from English: compare the time required to pronounce *e, be, beak, beach, beached.* Though the length of Latin syllables might vary considerably, as in these English examples, the Romans thought in terms of only two grades, short and long; a long syllable was felt to take about twice as long to pronounce as a short syllable (in musical terms, one might compare the half note and the quarter note). Latin quantitative meter is based upon the patterned alternation of long and short syllables, and the second step in reading Latin poetry aloud is to read each verse metrically, with an eye (or one should say, an ear) to this quantitative rhythm.

With practice a student can read a Latin poem metrically at first sight. Beginning students, however, will need to learn the mechanics of scanning a line on paper, i.e., of marking the long and short syllables and separating off the feet in each verse (a "foot" is the smallest characteristic group of syllables in a particular rhythmical pattern, e.g., a short syllable followed by a long one constitutes a foot in iambic meter—a "verse" is the smallest characteristic grouping of feet in a particular meter, e.g., a series of five iambs is an iambic pentameter). Such scansion is a fairly mechanical matter and involves the following steps:

a. *Mark the long and short syllables using the macron (‾) and the breve (˘), respectively.* In your initial introduction to Latin pronunciation you learned to identify a syllable as either long or short (necessary for determining placement of the stress accent in ordinary Latin speech—see the appendix, pp. xvii-xviii): a syllable is long only if it contains a long vowel or a diphthong or if the vowel, though itself short, is followed by two or more consonants. In this last instance, when attempting to determine the quantity of a syllable occurring at the end of a word within a verse, you must take into account any consonants occurring at the beginning of the next word: thus *et errō* scans *ĕt ērrō*, but *et terrā* scans *ēt tērrā*. In the opening line of Vergil's *Aeneid, Arma virumque canō Trōiae quī prīmus ab ōrīs,* the long and short syllables would be marked as follows:

$$\text{Ārmă vĭrūmquĕ cănō Trōiae quī prīmŭs ăb ōrīs.}$$

When a word ended with a vowel or a diphthong or a vowel followed by *-m* and the following word began with a vowel or a diphthong or a vowel preceded by *h-*, the final syllable of the first word and the beginning syllable of the next were usually slurred together, or "elided," into a single syllable. The syllable resulting from such "elision" was usually treated as short, when both of the original, unelided syllables would have been short; where either or both of the unelided syllables would have been long, the elided syllable was long. In writing out your scansion, the elided syllables should be connected with a line and the macron or breve should be centered above the space between the two words, as illustrated in the third verse of the *Aeneid,* which contains two elisions:

$$\text{lītŏră. Mūltŭm ĭlle‿ĕt tērrīs iăctātŭs ĕt āltō}$$

Occasionally the conditions for elision will exist but the poet will choose for metrical or other purposes not to elide; this phenomenon is called "hiatus," from the Latin word for "gaping" or "yawning" (a very apt term, as the mouth would remain open from the vowel of the first word, across the brief intervening pause, and on through the vowel of the following word).

b. *Mark off the feet using the slash (/).* In order to do so, you must, of course, recognize the particular metrical pattern in which the poem is composed. Again, with practice you will be able to do this at sight; in this text, however, the particular meters employed are identified in the introduction to each unit and the first few lines of each selection are fully scanned. The four metrical patterns you will encounter are these:

i. *Hendecasyllabic* (Unit 1). An eleven-syllable line, as the name implies:

$$- - / - \smile \smile / - \smile / - \smile / - \overset{\scriptscriptstyle =}{}$$

or

$$- \smile$$

or

$$\smile -$$

Here, and in the other meters described below, the symbol [≝] indicates that either a long or a short syllable is permitted.

ii. *Dactylic Hexameter* (Units 2, 5, and 7). A six-foot line, with a dactyl ($- \smile \smile$) in the first five feet and a spondee ($- -$) in the sixth (the last syllable of the line, even if apparently short, was regarded as long due to the natural pause occurring at the end of each verse). In any of the first four feet, a spondee might be substituted for the characteristic dactyl, often with the intended effect of slowing down the movement of the line.

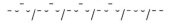

The first line of the *Aeneid* would be scanned as follows:

$$\text{Arma virumque canō Trōiae quī primus ab ōrīs.}$$

iii. *Alcaic Strophe* (Unit 3). A strophe is a stanza or characteristic group of verses of varying metrical pattern; the strophe is repeated any number of times in a lyric poem. The Alcaic Strophe is a four-line stanza following this pattern:

$$\text{≍ - ⌣ / - - / - ⌣ ⌣ / - ⌣ / -}$$
$$\text{≍ - ⌣ / - - / - ⌣ ⌣ / - ⌣ / -}$$
$$\text{≍ - ⌣ / - - / - ⌣ ⌣ / - ≍}$$
$$\text{- ⌣ ⌣ / - ⌣ ⌣ / - ⌣ / - ≍}$$

iv. *Elegiac Couplet* (Units 4 and 6). A metrical pattern common in epigrams and in elegiac and romantic poetry and consisting of alternating dactylic hexameter and pentameter lines in the following scheme:

$$\text{- ⌣ ⌣ / - ⌣ ⌣ / - ⌣ ⌣ / - ⌣ ⌣ / - ⌣ ⌣ / - -}$$

$$\text{- ⌣ ⌣ / - ⌣ ⌣ / - // - ⌣ ⌣ / - ⌣ ⌣ / -}$$

c. *Mark the principal pause in each line, using a double slash (//).*
    In longer lines of verse, the rhythm was usually slowed by one or sometimes two major pauses that generally coincided with the close of some sense unit (i.e., the end of a phrase, a clause, or a sentence) and which, therefore, are often easily noted in a modern text by some mark of punctuation. More often than not the principal pause occurs within a foot, where it is called a "caesura," rather than at the end of a foot, where it is called a "diaeresis"; in fact, in classical Latin poetry, the majority of the word endings in a line are caesurae, or, to put it another way, most words begin in one foot and continue over into the next, a deliberate device intended to interweave the feet more closely and prevent a choppy, sing-song effect. The first three lines of Vergil's *Aeneid* are thus fully scanned (note that the second *i* in *Lāvīnia* is treated as a consonant):

$$\bar{-} \;\smile\; \overset{\prime}{\smile}\; \bar{-} \quad \smile\; \overset{\prime}{\smile}\;/\;\bar{-}// \;\bar{-}\overset{\prime}{/}\;\bar{-} \quad \bar{-}/\;\bar{-}\;\smile\;\overset{\prime}{\smile}/\;\bar{-}\;\bar{-}$$
Arma virumque canō Trōiae quī primus ab ōrīs.

$$\bar{-}\;\smile\overset{\prime}{\smile}/\bar{-} \quad \bar{-}/\bar{-} \quad \smile\;\smile\;/\bar{-}\;//\;\bar{-}/\bar{-}\;\smile\; \smile\;/\bar{-}\;\bar{-}$$
Ītaliam fātō profugus Lāvīniaque vēnīt

$$\bar{-}\;\smile\;\smile\;//\;\bar{-} \quad \bar{-}\overset{\prime}{/}\;\bar{-} \quad \bar{-}\;/\bar{-}\;//\bar{-}/\bar{-}\;\smile\;\overset{\prime}{\smile}/\;\bar{-}\;\bar{-}$$
lītora. Multum ille et terrīs iactātus et altō

Once you have worked out the scansion of a passage you are ready to read it aloud. We know that the Romans, while not ignoring the actual word accent, gave extra emphasis to the first long syllable of each foot in a verse (it is a peculiarity of Latin poetry that this verse accent, or "ictus," and the normal word accent did not always coincide). In reading aloud, therefore, you should stress the first long syllable of each foot as well as observing generally the long and short quantities and the principal pauses (i.e., the ends of phrases, clauses, and sentences). In this last regard, it may be noted that classical authors tended to avoid an excess of end-stopped lines in favor of enjambed or "run-on" lines; that is, instead of concluding each clause or sentence at the end of a verse, the sense was often carried over to the beginning or the middle of the following line, thus ensuring a more continuous flow. Accordingly, the reader should avoid an exaggerated pause at the end of a verse, unless it happens to coincide with the end of a sense unit.

3. *Expressive Reading*

The final step, and this is a challenge in reading English aloud as well as Latin, is to read expressively. The ancient poet, as we have noted already, wrote for recitation, to entertain a listening audience: the poetry recitation was a performance and, if successful, a moving one. Vergil would not have recited a book of his *Aeneid* in a sing-song monotone, but would have read dramatically, varying the tone of his voice to suit the mood and giving proper emphasis to key words and phrases. As you are completing each unit in this book, once you have translated and discussed a passage as well as worked out its scansion, you should read the passage aloud one last time, rhythmically and expressively, in order to approximate as nearly as possible the effect intended by the Roman poet.

Appendix: Syllabification, Syllable Quantity, Accentuation

The following procedures for syllabifying a Latin word and determining the quantity of its syllables and the placement of its accent apply to Latin prose but may be profitably reviewed in connection with an introduction to Latin verse.

1. *Syllabification:* A Latin word has as many syllables as it has vowels and diphthongs. To syllabify, divide

   a. between two vowels or between a vowel and a diphthong (*ae, oe, ei, ui, au, eu*)

      e.g., *eō: e/ō; meae: me/ae*

   b. before a single consonant

      e.g., *laudō: lau/dō; moneō: mo/ne/ō*

   c. before the last consonant, where there are two or more consonants, but *not* before the *h* of aspirates (*ch, ph, th*), nor between *q* and *u*, nor (except occasionally *in poetry*) between a stop (*b, c, d, g, p, t*) and a liquid (*l, r*)

      e.g., *esse: es/se; servāre: ser/vā/re*

      BUT *patria: pa/tri/a; philosophia: phi/lo/so/phi/a; atque: at/que*

2. *Syllable Quantity:* A syllable is long, i.e., takes longer to pronounce, if

   a. it contains a long vowel

      e.g., *amō:* mark the syllable long in this way: *a/mō̄*

   b. it contains a diphthong

      e.g., *meae: me/āē; laudō: lāū/dō̄*

   c. it ends with a consonant

      e.g., *puella: pu/ēl/la; vēnisset: vē/nīs/sēt*

3. *Accentuation:* In a Latin word of two or more syllables (as in English), one syllable was accented, i.e., pronounced with greater stress; in Latin the position of the accent was determined in strict accordance with the following rules:

   a. In a two syllable word, the first syllable is accented.

   e.g., *amō: á/mō; esse: és/se*

   b. In a word of three or more syllables, the next to last (penultimate) syllable is accented, *if it is long;* if the penult is short, the preceding syllable (the antepenult) is accented.

   e.g., *puella: pu/él/la; servāre: ser/vā/re;*

   Catullus: Ca/túl/lus

   BUT *moneō: mó/ne/ō; patria: pá/tri/a;*

   Catulus: Cá/tu/lus

LATIN POETRY

FOR THE BEGINNING STUDENT

UNIT ONE

CATULLUS: LESBIA'S SPARROW

Introduction

CATULLUS' LIFE AND WORKS

Catullus (Gaius Valerius Catullus, ca. 84-54 B.C.), Rome's first and most popular love poet, was born of a wealthy family in Verona, in the north Italian province of Cisalpine Gaul. As a young man, Catullus moved to Rome, most likely to work on a legal career; soon, however, he turned his attention to literary pursuits, composing at least the 113 poems that survive today before his premature death at the age of thirty.

The poems have been arranged, whether by Catullus himself or some later editor, into three groups: 1-60 are written in a variety of meters and deal with a variety of topics, some of them satirical, many of them love poems or on other personal themes; 61-68 are longer pieces, including a 408-line *epyllion,* or "miniature epic," on the wedding of Peleus and Thetis (64); 69-116 also include lyric, romantic, and satiric pieces, many of them very short and epigrammatic, all of them in the elegiac meter. In his opening poem, Catullus called upon his Muse to inspire him in the writing of verse that would endure beyond a single generation (1.10: *plus uno maneat perenne saeclo*), a prayer that has certainly been fulfilled.

THE LESBIA POEMS

About twenty-five of Catullus' poems vividly depict his relationship with a woman whom he calls Lesbia (after the Greek poetess, Sappho, from the island of Lesbos) but who may confidently be identified with Clodia, a wealthy, enchanting aristocrat, sister of Cicero's nemesis P. Clodius Pulcher. Although ten years younger than Clodia, whom he met while her husband Quintus Metellus Celer was governor of Cisalpine Gaul, Catullus fell passionately and hopelessly in love with the woman, for she was both many-talented and beautiful. The Lesbia poems trace vividly the young man's initial infatuation, his happiness at the height of the romance, and his final bitter disillusionment at Clodia's eventual infidelity. The affair, begun perhaps in 59 B.C., is alluded to in poems dating as late as 55 or 54 B.C. Catullus died shortly thereafter, of a broken heart, as some romantically suppose.

The two poems presented here (Catullus 2 and 3) describe Clodia's affection for her pet sparrow and date to the earliest period of the love affair; the meter of both is hendecasyllabic.

Catullus 2

"Passer, dēliciae meae puellae,   1

quīcum lūdere, quem in sinū tenēre,   2

cui prīmum digitūm dare appetentī   3

et ācrīs solet incitāre morsūs,   4

cum dēsīderiō meō nitentī   5

cārum nescio quid lubet iocārī   6

(et sōlāciolum suī dolōris,   7

crēdō, ut tum gravis acquiescat ardor),   8

tēcum lūdere sīcut ipsa possem   9

et tristīs animī levāre cūrās!   10

1   **passer, passeris, M.**: sparrow (or some other small bird).
    dēliciae, dēliciārum, F. pl.: pet, darling.
    meae puellae: here and elsewhere in his poetry Catullus uses
        this expression for his girlfriend Lesbia.

2   **quīcum = quōcum**: "with whom."
    lūdō, lūdere, lūsī, lūsum: to play; complementary infinitive
        (like **tenēre, dare**, and **incitāre**) with **solet** (line 4).
    sinus, sinūs, M.: lap, bosom.

3   **digitus, digitī, M.**: finger; with **prīmum**, "fingertip."
    appetentī: "eager"; modifies **cui** (adjective and noun, or
        pronoun, were often widely separated in Latin
        verse—cf. **ācrīs . . . morsūs**, line 4).

4   **ācrīs = ācrēs**, acc. pl.
    soleō, solēre, solitus sum: to be accustomed to.
    incitō, incitāre, incitāvī, incitātum: to provoke.
    morsus, morsūs, M.: bite.

5   **cum**, conjunction: when, whenever.
    dēsīderium, dēsīderiī, N.: desire, longing; loved one.
    nitentī: "shining," "beautiful."

6   **cārus, -a, -um**: dear, precious.
    nescio quid: "something."
    lubet = libet, libēre, libuit, impersonal verb: it pleases; takes
        a dative object (here, **dēsīderiō**)
    iocārī: "to tease," "to play with."

7   **sōlāciolum, sōlāciolī, N.**: bit of comfort; sc. **es**.
    dolor, dolōris, M.: pain (of love).

8   **crēdō, crēdere, crēdidī, crēditum**: to trust; here par-
        enthetical.
    ut, conjunction: so that.
    acquiescat: "may become quiet."
    ardor, ardōris, M.: heat of passion.

9   **sīcut**, conjunction: just as.
    ipsa: "your mistress" (literally, "she herself").
    possem: "would that I might be able" (takes complementary
        infinitive).

10   **tristis, triste**: sad, grim; **tristīs = tristēs**, acc. pl.
    levō, levāre, levāvī, levātum: to alleviate, lighten.

Catullus 3

Lūgēte, ō Venerēs Cupīdinēsque,	1
et quantum est hominum venustiōrum!	2
Passer mortuus est meae puellae,	3
passer, dēliciae meae puellae,	4
quem plūs illa oculīs suīs amābat.	5
Nam mellītus erat suamque nōrat	6
ipsam tam bene quam puella mātrem;	7
nec sēsē ā gremiō illius movēbat,	8
sed circumsiliēns modo hūc modo illūc	9
ad sōlam dominam ūsque pīpiābat;	10
quī nunc it per iter tenēbricōsum	11
illud, unde negant redīre quemquam.	12

Birds drinking from a basin, eyed by a domestic cat; from a Pompeiian mosaic (Naples; photo, James C. Anderson, Jr.).

1   **lūgeō, lūgēre, lūxī, lūctum:** to mourn, lament.
     Venerēs Cupīdinēsque: "Venuses and Cupids" (i.e., the feminine and masculine powers of love and desire).

2   **venustus, -a, -um:** charming, blessed by Venus.
     quantum est hominum venustiōrum: "all the company of more charming men."

3   **mortuus est:** "has died."

5   **plūs,** comparative adverb: more.
     oculus, oculī, M.: eye (here, abl. of comparison).

6   **mellītus, -a, -um:** honeyed, or "a honey."
     nōrat = **nōverat,** from **noscō, noscere, nōvī, nōtum:** to know.
     Poets dropped the ve or vi out of perfect system verb forms whenever necessary to fit the meter of the poem; this was not merely "poetic license" but a reflection of the pronunciation of conversational Latin.

7   **suus, -a, -um:** his (own), her (own), its (own), their (own).
     ipsam: "mistress" (with **suam**).
     tam . . . quam: as . . . as.
     puella mātrem: sc. **noscit.**

8   **sēsē:** emphatic for **sē,** "itself."
     gremium, gremiī, N.: lap.

9   **circumsiliēns:** "hopping around."
     modo hūc modo illūc: "now this way, now that."

10   **ūsque,** adverb: continually.
     pīpiō, pīpiāre, pīpiāvī, pīpiātum: to chirp.

11   **eō, īre, iī, itum:** to go.
     iter, itineris, N.: journey.
     tenēbricōsus, -a, -um: dark, shadowy.

12   **unde,** adverb: from where.
     negō, negāre, negāvī, negātum: to deny, to say that . . . not.
     quemquam: acc. of **quisquam, quaequam, quidquam,** anyone, anything.
     redeō, redīre, rediī, reditum: to return.

At vōbīs male sit, malae tenēbrae 13

Orcī, quae omnia bella dēvorātis: 14

tam bellum mihi passerem abstulistis. 15

Ō factum male! Ō miselle passer! 16

Tuā nunc operā meae puellae 17

flendō turgidulī rubent ocellī. 18

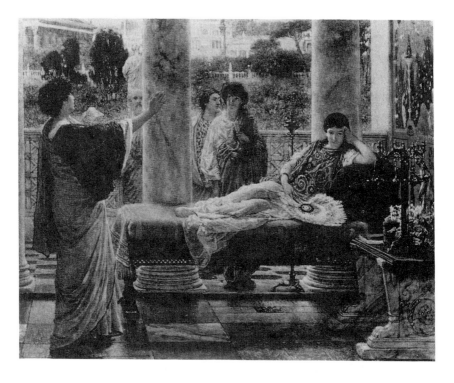

"At Lesbia's," by the Dutch painter Sir Lawrence Alma-Tadema, 1870
(private collection, England; photo, courtesy Sotheby's).

13 **at,** conjunction: but.
    male, adverb: badly, ill.
    sit: "may it be" or "may it go" (with **male,** a common curse
        in Latin).
    tenēbrae, tenēbrārum, F. pl.: darkness.
14 **Orcus, Orcī,** M.: Orcus or Pluto, ruler of the Underworld.
    bellus, -a, -um: beautiful.
    dēvorō, dēvorāre, dēvorāvī, dēvorātum: to devour.
15 **mihi:** dat. of reference (Catullus assumes the position of the
        mourner), "to my great loss."
    auferō, auferre, abstulī, ablātum: to take away.
16 **factum, factī,** N.: deed.
    male = malum.
    misellus, -a, -um: poor little (diminutive of **miser, -era,**
        -erum).
17 **opera, operae,** F.: deed (here abl. of cause).
18 **flendō:** "from weeping."
    turgidulus, -a, -um: swollen little (diminutive of **turgidus**).
    rubeō, rubēre: to be red.
    ocellus, ocellī, M.: diminutive of **oculus.**

Comprehension Questions

CATULLUS 2

1. What is Lesbia accustomed to doing with her sparrow?
2. When does the woman play with the sparrow?
3. What effects does the bird have on the woman's passion?
4. What does Catullus wish for?

CATULLUS 3

1. Whom does Catullus call upon to mourn?
2. What has happened to the sparrow?
3. How much did the woman love the bird?
4. Why did she love it so?
5. Where does the sparrow go?
6. What has happened to Lesbia's eyes?

Another of Catullus' best known poems is the brief poem 85:

Odi et amo. Quare id faciam, fortasse requiris?
Nescio, sed fieri sentio et excrucior.

> I hate and love: you'll ask perhaps, How can this be?
> I know not, but sense it's so and suffer agony.
>
> R.A.L.

UNIT TWO

VERGIL'S *AENEID:* DIDO ABANDONED

Introduction

VERGIL'S LIFE AND WORKS

Publius Vergilius Maro, "Vergil" as we call him today, was born in 70 B.C. near Mantua in northern Italy. In his youth he moved to Cremona, Milan, and finally to Rome for his education; he studied, among other subjects, rhetoric, medicine, astronomy, and Epicurean philosophy. In Rome, Vergil became acquainted with the poet Horace and the wealthy and influential Maecenas, a patron of several writers and artists of the period. With Maecenas' support he was able to spend his time in studying and writing. Vergil's first recognized work, a collection of pastoral poems known as the *Eclogues,* was published in 37 B.C. His next major work, the *Georgics,* was written at the request of, and in honor of, Maecenas and the young statesman Octavian, the future emperor Augustus; this work treated in four parts the agricultural activities of cultivating crops, including fruit trees and vines, of raising farm animals, and of beekeeping, and praised the ennobling virtues of life and work in the country.

At the urging of Augustus, Vergil devoted what were to be the last ten years of his life to creating an epic poem in celebration of Rome's greatness as a nation and an imperial power. Although Vergil died in 19 B.C., before his work on this epic was totally completed, his friends and literary executors saw to it that the poem was published. The *Aeneid,* or "Tale of Aeneas," in twelve books totalling more than 10,000 verses in dactylic hexameter, became for Rome what the *Iliad* and *Odyssey* were for the Greeks.

VERGIL'S STORY OF THE ADVENTURES OF AENEAS

After a long war, the ancient city of Troy was destroyed by the Greeks using the strategy of the wooden horse. The young prince Aeneas became leader of a group of refugees who sailed

11

12

away from Troy in search of a new homeland. After several years of sailing around the Mediterranean, the Trojans at last approached Italy, their ultimate goal; however, a great storm unleashed by Aeolus, king of the winds, at the instigation of the Trojans' nemesis, Juno, drove their ships aground near the north African city of Carthage. Dido, foundress and queen of Carthage, graciously accepted them into her city and then fell passionately in love with Aeneas; the two spent an entire year together and Dido considered the Trojan prince to be her husband. But Jupiter had ordained that the Trojans must settle only in Italy, and so he sent Mercury to inform Aeneas that he must leave Carthage.

The selection from the *Aeneid* that you will read here is found in the last lines of Book 4. Aeneas, prompted by the god Mercury, has just sailed away from Carthage in pursuit of his destiny. Abandoned, angry, and confused, Dido considers the possibilities open to her. She can follow after Aeneas; she can attack him with her fleet; she can meekly accept one of her former suitors from a nearby land. Proclaiming that she will try to forget Aeneas, she constructs a huge pyre and piles on it all the things Aeneas has left behind that remind her of him. In the reading you will learn of her final decision.

Vergil *Aeneid* 4.651-66

"Dulcēs exuviae, dum Fāta deusque sinēbat,   1

accipite hanc animam, mēque hīs exsolvite cūrīs.   2

Vīxī, et quem dederat cursum fortūna perēgī,   3

et nunc magna meī sub terrās ībit imāgō.   4

Urbem praeclāram statuī; mea moenia vīdī;   5

ulta virum poenās inimīcō ā frātre recēpī   6

fēlīx, heu nimium fēlīx—sī lītora tantum   7

numquam Dardaniae tetigissent nostra carīnae!"   8

1   **dulcis, dulce:** sweet, dear, beloved.
    exuviae, exuviārum, F. pl.: relics, spoils.
    dum, conjunction: while, as long as.
    sinō, sinere, sīvī, situm: to allow, permit.
2   **anima, animae,** F.: life, soul.
    hīs . . . cūrīs: "from these cares"; adjective and noun were
       often separated in Latin verse.
    exsolvō, exsolvere, exsolvī, exsolūtum: to release, free.
3   **vīvo, vīvere, vīxī, victum:** to live.
    quem: with **cursum,** "the journey which."
    cursus, cursūs, M.: course, journey.
    peragō, peragere, perēgī, perāctum: to carry out, finish.
4   **eō, īre, iī, itum:** to go.
    magna: modifies **imāgō** (see note on **hīs . . . cūrīs,** 2).
    imāgō, imāginis, F.: image, likeness, ghost.
5   **praeclārus, -a, -um:** famous, splendid.
    statuō, statuere, statuī, statūtum: to build, found.
    moenia, moenium, N. pl.: walls.
6   **ulta:** "having avenged."
    virum: Sychaeus, Dido's first husband, who was killed by
       her brother.
    inimīcus, -a, -um: unfriendly.
    recipiō, recipere, recēpī, receptum: to receive; with **poenam,**
       "to exact a penalty."
7   **fēlīx, fēlīcis:** happy, fortunate.
    heu, interjection: alas!, oh!
    nimium, adverb: too, too much.
    sī . . . tantum: "if only."
    lītus, lītoris, N.: shore, coast.
8   **numquam,** adverb: never.
    Dardanius, -a, -um: Trojan (Dardanus was the name of the
       founder of the Trojan line).
    tetigissent: "had touched," "had arrived at."
    nostra: modifies **lītora** (7).
    carīna, carīnae, F.: ship.

Dīxit, et ōs impressa torō, "Moriēmur inultae,   9

sed moriāmur," ait. "Sīc, sīc iuvat īre sub umbrās.   10

Hauriat hunc oculīs ignem crūdēlis ab altō   11

Dardanus, et nostrae sēcum ferat ōmina mortis."   12

Dīxerat, atque illam media inter tālia ferrō   13

conlāpsam aspiciunt comitēs, ēnsemque cruōre   14

spūmantem sparsāsque manūs. It clāmor ad alta   15

ātria: concussam bacchātur Fāma per urbem.   16

9   **ōs impressa torō:** "pressing her face to the couch."

       moriēmur: "we shall die"; note the use of the royal plural.

       inultus, -a, -um: unavenged.

10   **moriāmur:** "let us die."

       ait: "she says."

       iuvat: "it pleases (me)."

       umbra, umbrae, F.: the shades, the underworld (in the plural).

11   **hauriat:** "let (**Dardanus** is the subject) draw in, see."

       ignis, ignis, M.: fire.

       crūdēlis, crūdēle: cruel.

       altus, -a, -um: deep; as a noun, N., the sea, the deep.

12   **Dardanus:** "the Trojan."

       sēcum: "with him."

       ferat: "let him take."

       ōmen, ōminis, N.: sign, omen.

13   **media inter tālia:** "in the midst of such things."

       ferrō: "on the sword."

14   **conlāpsam:** "fallen," "collapsed."

       aspiciō, aspicere, aspexī, aspectum: to behold, see.

       comes, comitis, C.: companion, attendant.

       ēnsis, ēnsis, M.: sword.

       cruor, cruōris, M.: blood, gore.

15   **spūmantem:** "foaming," "frothing."

       sparsās: "spattered."

       it: "arises" (from **eō**, above line 4).

16   **ātrium, ātriī, N.:** hall, court.

       concussam: "shaken," "alarmed."

       bacchātur: "runs wildly."

Aeneid **4.667-92:** Dido's sister, Anna, hears the tragic news, rushes to the queen's side, and embraces her as she is dying. Here at the close of the book Juno acts to set Dido's spirit free from her body by sending the goddess Iris to cut off a lock of her hair as an offering to the gods of the underworld.

Aeneid 4.693-705

Tum Iūnō omnipotēns longum miserāta dolōrem	17
difficilīsque obitūs Īrim dēmīsit Olympō	18
quae luctantem animam nexōsque resolveret artūs.	19
Nam quia nec fātō meritā nec morte perībat,	20
sed misera ante diem subitōque accēnsa furōre,	21
nōndum illī flāvum Prōserpina vertice crīnem	22
abstulerat Stygiōque caput damnāverat Orcō.	23
Ergō Īris croceīs per caelum rōscida pinnīs	24

17 **Iūnō, Iūnōnis,** F.: Juno, wife of Jupiter and queen of the
  gods.
  omnipotēns: all powerful, omnipotent.
  miserāta: "pitying."
  dolor, dolōris, F.: pain; suffering.
18 **difficilīs = difficilēs,** acc. pl.
  obitus, obitūs, M.: death.
  Īris, Īridis, F.: Iris, the rainbow goddess and messenger of
  Juno. *Īrim* is acc. sing.
  Olympus, Olympī, M.: Mt. Olympus, the home of the Greek
  gods. Here abl., place from which.
19 **luctantem:** "struggling."
  nexōs . . . artūs: "tightly locked limbs."
  resolveret: "might release," "might set free."
20 **quia,** conjunction: since.
  meritus, -a, -um: deserved, proper (with **morte**).
  perībat: "she was perishing."
21 **subitus, -a, -um:** sudden, unexpected.
  accēnsa: "inflamed," "set on fire."
  furor, furōris, M.: madness.
22 **nōndum,** adverb: not yet.
  illī: "for her," or, with **vertice,** "from her head."
  flāvus, -a, -um: golden, yellow.
  Prōserpina, Prōserpinae, F.: Proserpina, wife of Pluto and
  goddess of the dead.
  vertex, verticis, M.: top of the head, head.
  crīnis, crīnis, M.: hair, lock of hair.
23 **auferō, auferre, abstulī, ablātum:** to remove, carry off.
  Stygius, -a, -um: of the Styx (a river in the Underworld),
  Stygian.
  damnō, damnāre, damnāvī, damnātum: to condemn, con-
  secrate as a sacrifice.
  Orcus, Orcī, M.: Orcus or Pluto, the god of the Underworld.
24 **ergō,** adverb: therefore.
  croceus, -a, -um: saffron-colored, yellow.
  rōscidus, -a, -um: dewy, moistened.
  pinna, pinnae, F.: feather, wing.

mīlle trahēns variōs adversō sōle colōrēs 25

dēvolat, et suprā caput astitit. "Hunc ego Dītī 26

sacrum iussa ferō, tēque istō corpore solvō." 27

Sīc ait, et dextrā crīnem secat; omnis et ūnā 28

dīlāpsus calor, atque in ventōs vīta recessit. 29

Vergil with the muses of history and tragedy; from a Tunisian mosaic (Mansell Collection).

25   **mīlle:** modifies **colōrēs.**

trahēns: ''drawing,'' ''trailing.''

adversō sōle: ''with the sun opposite.''

26   **dēvolō, dēvolāre, dēvolāvī, dēvolātum:** to fly down.

suprā, preposition with acc.: above, over.

astō, astāre, astitī: to stand, alight.

Dīs, Dītis, M.: Dis, another name for Orcus or Pluto.

27   **sacrum:** sc. **crīnem.**

ferō, ferre, tulī, lātum: to carry off.

iussa: modifies **ego,** ''ordered,'' ''having been ordered.''

iste, ista, istud: that, that of yours.

solvō, solvere, solvī, solūtum: to free, release.

28   **dextrā:** sc. **manū.**

secō, secāre, secuī, sectum: to cut off.

omnis et = et omnis.

ūnā, adverb: at the same time, at once.

29   **dīlāpsus:** sc. **est.** ''slipped away,'' ''vanished.''

calor, calōris, M.: warmth, heat (of the body).

ventus, ventī, M.: wind.

recēdō, recēdere, recessī, recessum: to disappear, withdraw.

Comprehension Questions

LINES 1-8

1. To what objects does Dido address her words in lines 1 and 2?
2. Where will her phantom go?
3. What accomplishments does Dido credit to herself?
4. Dido believes she would have remained happy had it not been for one circumstance. What was that?

LINES 9-16

1. What has Dido decided to do?
2. How will Aeneas learn of her death?
3. By what means does the queen end her life?
4. By whom are her actions discovered?
5. What is the reaction in her palace and in the city?
6. Who or what is Fama?

LINES 17-29

1. Why does Juno pity Dido?
2. Why is her death so slow?
3. What task does Juno assign Iris?
4. Why had Proserpina not yet consigned Dido's soul to the Underworld?
5. Comment on the sound effects in the second half of verse 29.

UNIT THREE

HORACE: THE CLEOPATRA ODE

Introduction

HORACE'S LIFE AND WORKS

One of the greatest poets of the "Golden Age" of Latin literature, during the rule of Caesar Augustus, was Quintus Horatius Flaccus. Horace, as he is known to English readers, was born in 65 B.C. in Venusia, a small town in southern Italy. Early on, his father, a former slave and a self-made man, decided to obtain for Horace the best education possible and so moved to Rome, the capital of the Empire. Horace never forgot his father's careful regard for his welfare nor the keen insights into life that his father would share as they walked to school together.

Some years later, when he was studying in Greece, Horace's fortunes took a downturn. This occurred in the aftermath of the assassination of Julius Caesar (on the Ides of March, 44 B.C.), when Horace, who had in 42 B.C. fought on the losing side in the war between Caesar's murderers and Octavian (Caesar's nephew and heir and the future emperor Augustus), returned to Italy to find his property confiscated. It was during this period that Horace began composing his *Satires,* which point out with wit and irony the weaknesses of man and society. Fortunately, this time of trouble did not last and in 38 B.C. Horace, through his friend the poet Vergil, was granted entrance into the "circle" of Maecenas, a wealthy patron of the arts and close advisor to Octavian.

With his financial and social situation thus secured, Horace began to have a new outlook on life. His work began to change too, as he turned his attention to Greek lyric, a highly personal, often self-revelatory kind of poetry. The result of this experiment, the *Odes* (or *Carmina*), occupied the largest part of the rest of the poet's life (he also wrote a collection of sometimes satiric, sometimes romantic *Epodes,* two books of *Epistles* in verse, and a very famous poem, the *Carmen Saeculare,* which was sung at a great centennial festival in 17 B.C. celebrating Rome and Augustus). Horace became a personal friend of the emperor and in several of his *Odes* showed his great support for the "new order" for Roman society undertaken by Augustus (which, by the way, was conducive to many elements of the poet's own philosophical temperament). Horace loved to write about the simple country life, easy living, balanced and rational thinking, good wine and good friends, and he often condemned extravagance and pretentiousness. His outlook might best be summarized in "Make the most of the moment (*carpe diem*), for life is short." He died in 8 B.C. and was buried with his friend Maecenas.

HORACE'S *ODE* 1.37: ON CLEOPATRA, QUEEN OF EGYPT

The year 31 B.C. was a very crucial one for the Roman world. In this year Octavian overcame the final opposition to his absolute control of the Empire when he defeated the combined forces of his former colleague Marcus Antonius and the alluring Egyptian queen Cleopatra in a sea battle off Actium in Greece. Antony and Cleopatra fled to Alexandria in Egypt, pursued by Octavian, where they met their deaths by suicide rather than be exposed to humiliation as captives in Octavian's public triumph at Rome. It was against this background that Horace composed this famous *Ode* on Cleopatra; the meter is the Alcaic strophe.

Horace *Odes* 1.37

Nunc est bibendum, nunc pede libero   1

pulsanda tellūs, nunc Saliāribus   2

ornāre pulvīnar deōrum   3

tempus erat dapibus, sodālēs.   4

1   **est bibendum:** "is the time for drinking" or "we must drink."

    līber,-era,-erum: free; here "carefree."

2   **pulsanda:** sc. **est;** "must be struck." With **tellus** as subject the phrase refers to dancing; freely, "let's dance."

    tellūs, tellūris, F.: earth, ground.

    Saliāris, Saliāre: Salian, of the Salii (modifies **dapibus** in line 4: adjective and noun were often widely separated in Latin poetry). The Salii were priests of the god Mars; their feasts were well-known for their lavishness.

3   **ornō, ornāre, ornāvī, ornātum:** to adorn, decorate; with **tempus erat.**

    pulvīnar, pulvīnāris, N.: a couch for the gods, set out with cushions at festive occasions. The gods were thought to be invisibly "present."

4   **dapis, dapis,** F.: a solemn feast, banquet.

    sodālis, sodālis, M.: companion; here "drinking companions."

Silver tetradrachm from Phoenicia picturing Marc Antony and Cleopatra VII, ca. 34 B.C. (photo, Fitzwilliam Museum, Cambridge).

For her beauty, as we are told, was in itself not altogether incomparable, nor such as to strike those who saw her; but converse with her had an irresistible charm, and her presence, combined with the persuasiveness of her discourse and the character which was somehow diffused about her behaviour towards others, had something stimulating about it.

Plutarch, *Life of Antony,* 27.2
Trans. B. Perrin

Antehāc nefās dēprōmere Caecubum 5
cellīs avītīs, dum Capitōliō 6
   rēgīna dēmentēs ruīnās 7
      fūnus et imperiō parābat 8

contāminātō cum grege turpium 9
morbō virōrum, quidlibet impotēns 10
   spērāre fortūnāque dulcī 11
      ēbria. Sed minuit furōrem 12

5   **antehāc,** adverb: before this, formerly; scanned as a disyllable (with the **e** barely sounded).

nefās, indeclinable noun: an impiety; sc. **erat.**

dēprōmō, dēprōmere, dēprōmpsī, dēprōmptum: to bring out,
carry out.

Caecubus, -a, -um: Caecuban; sc. **vīnum.** Caecubum was a
plain of Latium (the district around Rome) famous for
its wine.

6   **cella, cellae,** F.: storeroom, cellar.

avītus, -a, -um: ancestral (literally, "of a grandfather,"
avus).

Capitōlium, Capitōliī, N.: the Capitoline, one of the seven
hills of Rome and the site of the temple of Jupiter
Optimus Maximus; here, symbolic of Roman power.

7   **rēgīna, rēgīnae,** F.: queen. The reference is to Cleopatra
VII, Queen of Egypt; despised by the Romans, she is
never referred to by name in Augustan verse.

dēmēns, dēmentis: out of one's mind, mad, demented.

ruīna, ruīnae, F.: downfall, ruin.

8   **fūnus, fūneris,** N.: burial procession, funeral, death; **fūnus et**
= **et fūnus.**

imperium, imperiī, N.: dominion, empire.

9   **contāminātus, -a, -um:** fouled, contaminated; modifies **grege.**

grex, gregis, M.: herd, flock; here refers contemptuously to
the eunuchs in Cleopatra's palace.

turpis, turpe: dirty, foul, morally unclean.

10   **morbum, morbī,** N.: disease, sickness, vice; abl. of cause
with **turpium.**

quīlibet, quaelibet, quidlibet: anyone, anything.

impotēns, impotentis: powerless, out of control, insane.

11   **spērō, spērāre, spērāvī, spērātum:** to hope for, expect; com-
plementary infinitive with **impotēns.**

dulcis, dulce: sweet, kind.

12   **ēbrius, -a, -um:** drunken, inebriated.

minuō, minuere, minuī, minūtum: to lessen, diminish.

furōr, furōris, M.: madness, furor, frenzy.

vix ūna sospes nāvis ab ignibus,   13

mentemque lymphātam Mareōticō   14

redēgit in vērōs timōrēs   15

Caesar, ab Ītaliā volantem   16

rēmīs adurgēns, accipiter velut   17

mollēs columbās aut leporem citus   18

vēnātor in campīs nivālis   19

Haemoniae, daret ut catēnīs   20

Augustus in military regalia (Vatican; photo, James C. Anderson, Jr.).

13   **vix,** adverb: hardly, scarcely.

    sospes, sospitis: saved, unhurt; the reference is to the battle of Actium.

14   **mēns, mentis, F.:** mind, spirit.

    lymphātus, -a, -um: frantic, raging.

    Mareōticus, -a, -um: Mareotic; sc. **vīnō.** The district around Lake Mareotis in Lower (northern) Egypt was well known for its sweet wines.

15   **redigō, redigere, redēgī, redāctum:** to drive, lead back.

16   **Caesar, Caesaris, M.:** Caesar Octavianus, the nephew and heir of Julius Caesar.

    volantem: "fleeing or "as she fled"; sc. **rēgīnam.**

17   **rēmus, rēmī, M.:** oar; here, by metonymy (using a part of something to indicate the whole), referring to the ships of Octavian.

    adurgēns: "pursuing closely"; modifies **Caesar.**

    accipiter, accipitris, M.: a hawk, falcon; sc. **adurget,** "pursues."

    velut: as; introduces a simile to picture more vividly the scene described.

18   **mollis, molle:** tender, soft, gentle.

    columba, columbae, F.: dove.

    lepus, leporis, M.: hare.

    citus, -a, -um: swift, fast.

19   **venātor, venātōris, M.:** hunter; sc. **adurget.**

    campus, campī, M.: field, plain.

    nivālis, nivāle: snowy, snow-covered.

20   **Haemonia, Haemoniae, F.:** Thessaly, a mountainous district on the east coast of Greece.

    daret ut: "so that he (the hunter) might give"; a subjunctive clause of purpose.

    catēna, catēnae, F.: chain. Prisoners of war were forced to march in chains in a Roman triumph (a victory procession).

fātāle mōnstrum. Quae generōsius	21
perīre quaerēns nec muliēbriter	22
expāvit ēnsem nec latentēs	23
classe citā reparāvit ōrās.	24
Ausa et iacentem vīsere rēgiam	25
vultū serēnō, fortis et asperās	26
tractāre serpentēs, ut ātrum	27
corpore combiberet venēnum,	28

Fragment of a relief from Praeneste depicting a Roman gallery of the Augustan period; the crocodile symbolizes Octavian's conquest of Egypt (Vatican; photo, Robert I. Curtis).

21   **quae = illa.**
    fātālis, fātāle: deadly, fatal.
    mōnstrum, mōnstrī, N.: a wonder, something abnormal, a
       monster.
    generōsius, comparative adverb: "more nobly."
22   **pereō, perīre, periī, peritum:** to pass away, perish.
    quaerēns: "seeking"; modifies **quae.**
    nec . . . nec (line 23): neither . . . nor.
    muliēbriter, adverb: in the manner of a woman (**mulier,
       mulieris, F.**).
23   **expavescō, expavescere, expāvī:** to dread.
    ēnsis, ēnsis, M.: sword.
    latentēs: "hidden"; modifies **ōrās.**
24   **classis, classis, F.:** fleet (of ships).
    reparō, reparāre, reparāvī, reparātum: to acquire again, re-
       cover, seek.
25   **ausa:** sc. **est,** "she dared."
    et . . . et (line 26): both . . . and.
    iacentem: "fallen," "destroyed."
    vīso, vīsere, vīsī, vīsum: to look at carefully, contemplate.
    rēgia, rēgiae, F.: royal palace.
26   **vultus, vultūs, M.:** face, visage, countenance.
    serēnus, -a, -um: bright, serene.
    fortis et = et fortis.
    asperus, -a, -um: harsh, vicious.
27   **tractō, tractāre, tractāvī, tractātum:** to hold, handle.
    serpēns, serpentis, C.: serpent, snake.
    ut . . . combiberet (line 28): "so that she might drink in."
    āter, -tra, -trum: black, deadly.
28   **venēnum, venēnī, N.:** poison.

dēlīberātā morte ferōcior;   29

saevīs Liburnīs scīlicet invidēns   30

  prīvāta dēdūcī superbō   31

    nōn humilis mulier triumphō.   32

Augustan denarius celebrating the capture of Egypt, 28 B.C. (photo, courtesy American Numismatic Society, New York).

29   **dēlīberātus, -a, -um:** decided upon, determined.

       ferōx, ferōcis: bold, fierce.

30   **saevus, -a, -um:** raging mad, fierce, cruel.

       Liburnus, -a, -um: Liburnian; sc. **nāvibus.** Liburnian galleys, developed by the Liburnians in northwest Greece, were swift ships used by Octavian's forces at Actium.

       scīlicet, parenthetical adverb: you may be sure, certainly.

       invidēns: "despising," "refusing"; takes **dēdūcī** as object.

31   **prīvātus, -a, -um:** private, not official (i.e., no longer queen).

       dēdūcō, dēdūcere, dēdūxī, dēductum: to lead off.

       superbus, -a, -um: lofty, arrogant; modifies **triumphō** in the next verse.

32   **humilis, humile:** humble, meek, submissive.

       triumphus, triumphī, M.: a triumph (see note on **catēna,** line 20); **triumphō = ad triumphum.**

Comprehension Questions

LINES 1-12

1. What three things does Horace call on his companions to do?
2. Why would these activities have been wrong earlier?
3. What had the queen been planning?
4. What sort of picture does Horace give of Cleopatra at first?

LINES 12-21

1. What causes the queen to "sober up"?
2. Whom does Horace compare to a "hawk" and a "hunter"?
3. To what does he compare Cleopatra?

LINES 21-32

1. How did the queen die, according to this poem?
2. What was the alternative to her suicide?
3. Identify at least six words in this section of the poem that suggest Cleopatra's courage and determination.

UNIT FOUR

OVID'S *FASTI:*
THE LEGEND OF ROMULUS AND REMUS

Introduction

OVID'S LIFE AND WORKS

Ovid (Publius Ovidius Naso), the most famous of the Roman elegiac poets, was a younger contemporary of Vergil and thus a poet of the Augustan Age, a period of thriving artistic creativity. He was born of an equestrian family in the small, central Italian town of Sulmo in 43 B.C., but moved to Rome as a young man to be in the center of culture and to associate himself with other poets of the day. Although trained to be a lawyer and a government official, as a good staunch Roman should be, Ovid preferred writing poetry and soon turned his attention entirely to that pursuit. He was married three times and had one child, a daughter.

Ovid's poetry, while much influenced by Catullus, Vergil, and Horace (whom he knew personally), was in many ways quite original. He composed a great many books of poems in a wide variety of types and themes. Much of his work was in the genre of elegiac poetry, often serious verse written in a meter (the elegiac couplet) similar to the epic hexameters of Vergil, but shorter pieces on personal themes, usually treated in a witty and sophisticated manner. Several of his poetry books are almost exclusively concerned with romantic love, especially one collection known as the *Amores* ("Affairs of Love"). Another, the *Ars Amatoria* ("The Art of Love"), is more clever than sentimental, and is something like a singles handbook. It was intended to be amusing, but it seems that some Romans, including perhaps the emperor Augustus, found it vulgar. Augustus was trying to improve the state of morality in Rome and this book may have been offensive enough to have been one cause of Ovid's banishment to Tomi on the Black Sea in A.D. 8; despite the poet's repeated pleas, he was never pardoned and died in exile in A.D. 17.

During his banishment Ovid continued to write poetry. He hated his exile at Tomi, and his collections of poems known as the *Tristia* ("Lamentations") and the *Epistulae ex Ponto* ("Letters from Pontus") show his grim perspective on life far from Rome, friends, and family. Ovid's more melancholy side can also be seen in the *Heroides,* a unique set of poems written in the form of letters from women to their hero lovers, which give, for a change, the women's side of the story.

But Ovid is best known for the *Metamorphoses,* a poem of epic proportions and his only surviving work in dactylic hexameter. In this poem Ovid retells numerous myths of transformation, artfully connected and chronologically arranged beginning with the transformation of chaos into an ordered universe and concluding with the metamorphosis of Julius Caesar into a god. A selection from the *Metamorphoses,* one of the best sources we have for the ancient Greek and Roman myths, is included as the next unit in this text.

A similar collection, written at about the same time as the *Metamorphoses* (beginning around A.D. 2), is the *Fasti.* This long poem, a sort of calendar in verse in six books for the months January through June (the books for the remaining six months were either never completed or have been lost), is also a collection of myths and legends, but with a different purpose. These are all stories that tell about the origins of Roman holidays, the legendary events that took place in the dawn of Rome's history and were preserved in the rituals and observations of public occasions still practiced in Rome in classical times. This poem provides a tremendous amount of information about Roman customs and habits of daily life, because, of course, religious practices were a much more integral facet of Roman life than they are today. The selection given here is from that poem, and tells part of the story behind the celebration in honor of the deified Romulus; the meter is the elegiac couplet.

ROMULUS AND REMUS: THE FOUNDING OF ROME

In the beginning of his *History of Rome,* the historian Livy, who lived at the same time as Vergil and Ovid, gives one version of the story of Romulus and Remus and how Rome came to be founded. The poet Ovid recounts another version in Book 4 of the *Fasti,* the book for the month of April. According to legend, Romulus and Remus were the twin sons of the princess Rhea Silvia and the Roman war god, Mars, and thus the grandsons of Numitor, the eighth-century B.C. king of the important Italian city of Alba Longa. When the boys were only infants, their wicked great-uncle Amulius overthrew and imprisoned his brother Numitor, murdered Rhea Silvia, and tried to remove the twins from the line of succession by having servants drown them in the nearby Tiber River. Amulius' plot was foiled, however, by destiny, as legend would have it: a she-wolf found the boys on a bank where they had been left by receding flood waters and nursed them until they were rescued by a local shepherd, who took them home to his wife to raise. They grew up, discovered their true identity and their right to kingship, freed Numitor and restored him to the throne at Alba Longa, and led off an expedition to found a new city in the hilly region near the Tiber River where they had been abandoned and rescued in their infancy. With the construction of the new city and its walls in progress, a dispute arose between the two brothers over the right to govern. In a fight that took place, according to legend, on the 21st of April, 753 B.C., Remus was slain, by his brother Romulus according to Livy's account, by Romulus' lieutenant, Celer, in Ovid's version. To Romulus fell sole rule of the city, which was thereafter called "Rome," after the name of its first king.

In the following excerpt we encounter the brothers Romulus and Remus just as the usurper Amulius has been put to death.

The "Capitoline Wolf," Etruscan bronze; the infants were added in the fifteenth century (Rome, Conservatori; photo, James C. Anderson, Jr.)

Ovid *Fasti* 4.809-18

Iam luerat poenās frāter Numitōris, et omne   1

pastōrum geminō sub duce vulgus erat.   2

Contrahere agrestēs et moenia pōnere utrīque   3

convenit; ambigitur moenia pōnat uter.   4

"Nil opus est" dīxit "certāmine" Rōmulus "ūllō;   5

māgna fidēs avium est: experiāmur avēs."   6

Rēs placet. Alter init nemorōsī saxa Palātī;   7

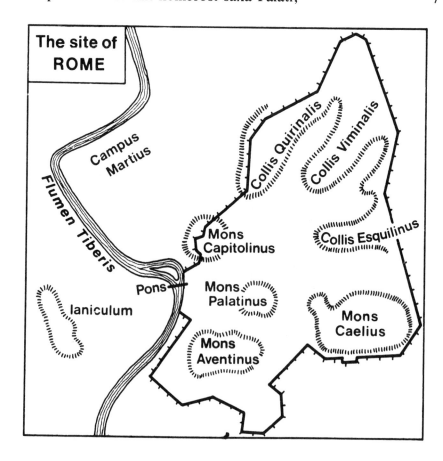

1   **luō, luere, luī:** to suffer; with **poenās,** "to pay the penalty (for a crime)."

    Numitor, Numitōris, M.: Numitor, king of Alba Longa and brother of Amulius.

    omne: modifies **vulgus** in verse 2; adjective and noun were often widely separated in Latin poetry.

2   **pastor, pastōris, M.:** shepherd.

    geminus, -a, -um: twin, double.

    duce: here the singular is employed where English would use the plural; or, translate "leadership."

    vulgus, vulgī, N.: crowd, populace; read with **pastōrum.**

3   **contrahō, contrahere, contraxī, contractum:** to draw together, unite.

    agrestis, agrestis, M.: rustic, peasant.

    moenia, moenium, N. pl.: walls, fortifications.

    utrīque convenit: "each agreed."

4   **ambigitur:** "the question was."

    pōnat: "should build" (i.e., should be in charge of the construction and thus of the city's foundation).

    uter, -tra, -trum: which of the two.

5   **nil opus est:** "there is no need of"; this phrase takes an ablative (of separation).

    certāmen, certāminis, N.: conflict, fight.

6   **fidēs, fideī, F.:** trust, faith, confidence.

    avis, avis, F.: bird; here refers to the auspices (**avis** + **spectō**), omens obtained from observing the flight of birds, an Etruscan method of divination. Translate, "in the auspices."

    experiāmur: "let us try" or "let us consult."

7   **placeō, placēre, placuī, placitum:** to please, be agreeable, be approved; here, and with several of the verbs below, the historical present is used.

    alter . . . alter (line 8): "the one . . . the other."

    init: "goes up onto."

    nemorōsus, -a, -um: wooded, forested.

    saxum, saxī, N.: rock, stone; sc. **ad** or **in.**

    Palātium, Palātī, N.: the Palatine hill, one of the seven hills of Rome.

alter Aventīnum māne cacūmen init.   8

Sex Remus, hic volucrēs bis sex videt ordine. Pāctō   9

stātur, et arbitrium Rōmulus urbis habet.   10

Fasti **4.819-26:** The work of building the new fortifications is begun, performed with all due pomp and religious ritual. Romulus concludes the ceremony with a prayer to the gods.

Fasti **4.827-52**

Vōx fuit haec rēgis: "Condentī, Iūppiter, urbem,   11

et genitor Māvors Vestaque māter, ades,   12

quōsque pium est adhibēre deōs, advertite cūnctī.   13

Auspicibus vōbīs hoc mihi surgat opus.   14

Longa sit huic aetās dominaeque potentia terrae,   15

sitque sub hāc oriēns occiduusque diēs."   16

8   Aventīnus, -a, -um: of the Aventine, another of Rome's
         seven hills.
      māne, adverb: in the morning.
      cacūmen, cacūminis, N.: summit; sc. ad or in.
9   hic: i.e., Romulus.
      volucris, volucris, F.: bird.
      bis, adverb: twice.
      ordō, ordinis, M.: order, rank, formation; sc. in.
      pāctum, pāctī, N.: mutual agreement, compact.
10   stātur: "the matter is resolved."
      arbitrium, arbitriī, N.: authority, rule.
11   condentī: "as I am dedicating."
      Iūppiter, Iovis, M.: Jupiter, sky-god and chief deity of the
         Romans.
12   genitor, genitōris, M.: father.
      Māvors, Māvortis, M.: another name for Mars, the god of
         war and father of Romulus and Remus.
      Vesta, Vestae, F.: Vesta, goddess of the hearth and protec-
         tress of Rome; according to legend the twins' mother
         was Rhea Silvia, a Vestal Virgin (priestess of Vesta).
      ades: "stand by me."
13   quōs . . . deōs: "whatever gods."
      pius, -a, -um: right, proper.
      adhibeō, adhibēre, adhibuī, adhibitum: to turn to, have
         present.
      advertō, advertere, advertī, adversum: to notice, pay atten-
         tion, take heed.
      cūnctus, -a, -um: all.
14   auspex, auspicis, C.: patron, supporter; here in ablative ab-
         solute with vōbīs.
      surgat: "let . . . arise."
15   sit: "let there be."
      aetās, aetātis, F.: age, span of time.
      domina, dominae, F.: mistress; here in apposition to terrae.
      potentia, potentiae, F.: power, dominance.
16   sub hāc: sc. potentiā.
      oriēns, orientis: rising; with diēs, eastern.
      occiduus, -a -um: falling, setting; western.

Ille precābātur. Tonitrū dedit ōmina laevō   17

    Iūppiter, et laevō fulmina missa polō.   18

Auguriō laetī, iaciunt fundāmina cīvēs,   19

    et novus exiguō tempore mūrus erat.   20

Hoc Celer urget opus, quem Rōmulus ipse vocārat,   21

    "sint" que "Celer, cūrae" dīxerat "ista tuae,   22

nēve quis aut mūrōs aut factam vōmere fossam   23

    trānseat; audentem tālia dēde necī."   24

Quod Remus ignōrāns humilēs contemnere mūrōs   25

    coepit et "Hīs populus" dīcere "tūtus erit?"   26

Nec mora, trānsiluit. Rūtrō Celer occupat ausum;   27

17 **precābātur:** "was praying."
 tonitrus, tonitrūs, M.: thunder.
 ōmen, ōminis, N.: sign, omen.
 laevus, -a, -um: on the left. Omens appearing to the left were
   generally regarded as favorable.
18 **fulmen, fulminis, N.:** lightning.
 polus, polī, M.: heavens, sky.
 missa: sc. **sunt.**
19 **augurium, auguriī, N.:** omen, portent.
 fundāmen, fundāminis, N.: foundation.
20 **exiguus, -a, -um:** short, slight.
 mūrus, mūrī, M.: wall.
21 **Celer, Celeris, M.:** Celer, Romulus' second in command.
 urgeō, urgēre, ursī: to urge on, press, encourage.
 opus, operis, N.: work.
 vocārat = vocāverat.
22 **sint . . . cūrae . . . ista tuae:** "let these things be your
   responsibility."
23 **nēve quis . . . trānseat** (24): "nor let anyone cross."
 factam: "made," "dug."
 vōmer, vōmeris, M.: plow.
 fossa, fossae, F.: ditch, trench; this refers to the pomerium, a
   plowed trench that marked as sacred the boundaries
   of the city.
24 **audentem tālia:** "anyone daring such things."
 dēdō, dēdere, dēdidī, dēditum: to give over, consign to.
 nex, necis, F.: death.
25 **quod = hoc** (acc.)
 ignōrāns: "not knowing"; modifies **Remus.**
 humilis, humile: humble, low, simple.
 contemnō, contemnere, contempsī, contemptum: to scorn,
   mock, belittle.
26 **coepit:** "he began."
 tūtus, -a, -um: safe.
27 **nec mora:** "without delay."
 trānsiliō, trānsilīre, trānsiluī: to leap across.
 rūtrum, rūtrī, N.: shovel.
 occupō, occupāre, occupāvī, occupātum: to seize, attack, kill.
 ausum: "the daring man."

ille premit dūram sanguinulentus humum. 28

Haec ubi rēx didicit, lacrimās intrōrsus obortās 29

dēvorat et clausum pectore vulnus habet. 30

Flēre palam nōn vult exemplaque fortia servat, 31

"Sīc" que "meōs mūrōs trānseat hostis" ait. 32

Dat tamen exsequiās; nec iam suspendere flētum 33

sustinet, et pietās dissimulāta patet. 34

Osculaque applicuit positō suprēma ferētrō 35

atque ait, "Invītō frāter adempte, valē." 36

Ovid deliberately recalls in these lines the conclusion of Catullus' elegy on the death of his brother (Catullus 101.6-10):

Heu miser indigne frater adempte mihi,
nunc tamen interea haec, prisco quae more parentum
tradita sunt tristi munere ad inferias,
accipe fraterno multum manantia fletu,
atque in perpetuum, frater, ave atque vale.

Alas, poor brother, wrongly robbed from me,
accept at least these grave-goods, my sad gifts
(by ancient custom) to the shades below,
gifts moistened with a brother's tears: and then
forever, brother, hail, and then . . . farewell.

R.A.L.

28 **premō, premere, pressī, pressum:** to press, lie upon.
sanguinulentus, -a, -um: bloody.
humus, humī, F.: ground.
29 **discō, discere, didicī:** to learn.
lacrima, lacrimae, F.: tear.
intrōrsus, adverb: within.
obortās: "arising."
30 **dēvorō, dēvorāre, dēvorāvī, dēvorātum:** to devour, repress, hold back.
clausus, -a, -um: shut in, enclosed.
pectus, pectoris, N.: breast, heart; sc. **in.**
vulnus, vulneris, N.: wound.
31 **fleō, flēre, flēvī, flētum:** to weep.
palam, adverb: openly.
vult: "he wishes."
exemplum, exemplī, N.: example.
32 **trānseat:** "let . . . cross" or "may . . . cross."
ait: "he says."
33 **exsequiae, exsequiārum, F. pl.:** funeral.
suspendō, suspendere, suspendī, suspēnsum: to hold back, repress.
flētus, flētūs, M.: weeping, lamentation.
34 **pietās, pietātis, F.:** piety, devotion, affection.
dissimulāta: "concealed."
pateō, patēre, patuī: to reveal, lay open.
35 **osculum, osculī, N.:** kiss.
applicō, applicāre, applicuī, applicātum: to press.
positō: "when it had been set in place."
suprēmus, -a, -um: last, final.
ferētrum, ferētrī, N.: bier; sc. **in.**
36 **invītus, -a, -um:** unwilling, not wanting it; sc. **mē** (abl. of separation).
adempte: "taken away"; voc., modifying **frāter.**

Comprehension Questions

LINES 1-10

1. Upon what two undertakings were Romulus and Remus agreed?
2. On what issue was there disagreement?
3. How did they decide to resolve the dispute?
4. What did the two brothers see?

LINES 11-24

1. What deities did Romulus invoke for their blessing?
2. What were his wishes for the new city?
3. What signs did Jupiter send?
4. What was Celer's responsibility and how was he to enforce it?

LINES 25-36

1. What did Remus ask about the walls and what did he do to them?
2. What was Celer's response?
3. Why did Romulus at first conceal his grief?
4. What was his final reaction?

UNIT FIVE

OVID'S *METAMORPHOSES:*
THE GOLDEN AGE

Introduction

OVID'S *METAMORPHOSES*

The Augustan poet Ovid, whose life and works are discussed in the Introduction to the preceding unit (p. 33), is probably most admired for his epic tale of changes, the *Metamorphoses,* a poem of some 12,000 dactylic hexameter verses (the only one of Ovid's surviving works in that meter). Each of the many stories recounted in this fifteen-book collection recounts some mythical mutation, beginning with the creation of the universe out of primordial chaos, ending with the metamorphosis of Julius Caesar (the reigning emperor Augustus' adoptive father) into a god, and including altogether about 250 interconnected myths of change, such as the transformation of the weaver Arachne into a spider and of the river nymph Daphne into a laurel tree. Early in Book One of the *Metamorphoses* Ovid tells of the world's degeneration, by stages, from a wondrous, Eden-like Golden Age into the corrupt Age of Iron.

THE GOLDEN AGE

The Greek poet Hesiod, who lived in the late eighth century B.C., wrote our earliest surviving account of this mythical Golden Age. In his *Works and Days,* Hesiod divided the Ages of Man into four periods, giving each the name of a metal—Gold, Silver, Bronze, and Iron; he imagined an Age of Heroes between the Bronze and Iron Ages and considered himself and those of his own day to be living in the Iron Age. In this scheme, the Golden Age was a paradise, a time of peace and leisure unlike the poet's own age, as Hesiod wrote (verses 109-20, in Lattimore's translation),

In the beginning, the immortals
who have their homes on Olympos

created the golden generation of mortal people.
These lived in Kronos' time, when he
  was the king of heaven.
They lived as if they were gods,
  their hearts free from sorrow,
by themselves, and without hard work or pain;
  no miserable
old age came their way; their hands, their feet,
  did not alter.
They took their pleasure in festivals,
  and lived without troubles.
When they died, it was as if they fell asleep.
  All goods
were theirs. The fruitful grainland
  yielded its harvest to them
of its own accord; this was great and abundant,
  while they at their pleasure
quietly looked after their works,
  in the midst of good things,
prosperous in flocks, on friendly terms
  with the blessed immortals.

Hesiod's tale of the Golden Age and his account of the world's decline through the Ages of Silver, Bronze, and Iron became favorite subjects for such Latin poets as Vergil (*Eclogue* 4, *Georgics* 1.121ff), Horace (*Epode* 16), Tibullus (1.3.35ff), and Juvenal (6.1ff), as well as for Ovid.

As you read the following passage from the *Metamorphoses,* you will notice many similarities between the treatments by Ovid and his predecessor Hesiod, who was writing some seven hundred years earlier. In your future reading of Latin verse, you may like to compare accounts of the mythological Golden Age by other Roman poets. In particular, it may interest you to see the way the satirist Juvenal (ca. A.D. 65-135), with his typical sardonic humor, treats the theme so differently from the idealized portrayals of Vergil, Ovid, and Tibullus.

Statue of Ovid in the town square at Sulmona (Sulmo; photo, James C. Anderson, Jr.).

Ovid *Metamorphoses* 1.89-112

‿ ‿‿/ ‿ ‿ ‿/ ‿ ‿/‿ // ‿/ ‿ ‿ ‿/ ‿ ‿
Aurea prīma sata est aetās, quae vindice nūllō,   1

‿ ‿ ‿/‿ // ‿ ‿/‿ ‿ ‿/ ‿ ‿/‿ ‿ ‿/‿ ‿
sponte suā, sine lēge fidem rēctumque colēbat.   2

‿ ‿ ‿ ‿/‿ ‿ ‿/‿ // ‿/ ‿ ‿ ‿/‿ ‿‿/ ‿ ‿
Poena metusque aberant, nec verba minantia fīxō   3

aere legēbantur nec supplex turba timēbat   4

iūdicis ōra suī, sed erant sine vindice tūtī.   5

Nōndum caesa suīs, peregrīnum ut vīseret orbem,   6

montibus in liquidās pīnus dēscenderat undās,   7

1 aureus, -a, -um: golden.
   serō, serere, sēvī, satum: to sow, beget, give birth to.
   aetās, aetātis, F.: age, generation.
   vindex, vindicis, M.: punisher, avenger.
2 suus, -a, -um: his (own), her (own), its (own); with sponte,
      "of its own will."
   fidēs, fideī, F.: faith, belief, confidence.
   rēctum, rēctī, N.: right, virtue.
   colō, colere, coluī, cultum: to till, cultivate, cherish.
3 poena, poenae, F.: punishment, penalty.
   metus, metūs, M.: fear.
   absum, abesse, āfuī: to be absent.
   minantia: "warning" (modifies verba).
   fixus, -a, -um: fixed, immovable.
4 aes, aeris, N.: bronze; Roman laws were posted in public
      places on bronze tablets.
   legō, legere, lēgī, lēctum: to choose, gather, read.
   supplex, supplicis: kneeling, suppliant.
   turba, turbae, F.: mob, crowd.
5 iūdex, iūdicis, M.: judge.
   ōs, ōris, N.: face, countenance, mouth.
   erant: sc. hominēs.
   tūtus, -a, -um: safe.
6 nōndum, adverb: not yet.
   caesa: "cut," "hewn"; modifies pīnus in line 7. Adjective
      and noun were often widely separated in Latin poetry
      (cf. suīs . . . montibus, peregrīnum . . . orbem, liquidās
      . . . undās, and nūlla . . . lītora, lines 6-8).
   peregrīnus, -a, -um: foreign, strange, exotic.
   vīso, vīsere, vīsī, vīsum: to visit, go to see.
   ut vīseret: "in order to visit."
   orbis, orbis, M.: region, territory, land.
7 pīnus, pīnī, F.: pine, or anything made of pine (here a boat).
   dēscendō, dēscendere, dēscendī, dēscēnsum: to descend.
   unda, undae, F.: wave.

nūllaque mortālēs praeter sua lītora nōrant.   8

Nōndum praecipitēs cingēbant oppida fossae;   9

nōn tuba dīrēctī, nōn aeris cornua flexī,   10

nōn galeae, nōn ēnsis erat: sine mīlitis ūsū   11

mollia sēcūrae peragēbant ōtia gentēs.   12

Ipsa quoque immūnis rāstrōque intācta nec ūllīs   13

saucia vōmeribus per sē dabat omnia tellūs;   14

contentīque cibīs nūllō cōgente creātīs   15

arbuteōs fētūs montānaque frāga legēbant   16

Among Ovid's models for his account of the Golden Age was Vergil's Fourth ("Messianic") *Eclogue,* which prophesied the birth of a child who would usher in a new Golden Age; there are several correspondences between the Ovid passage and these lines (37-41) from Vergil's poem:

hinc, ubi iam firmata virum te fecerit aetas,
cedet et ipse mari vector, nec nautica pinus
mutabit merces; omnis feret omnia tellus.
non rastros patietur humus, non vinea falcem;
robustus quoque iam tauris iuga solvet arator.

Thereafter, when now strengthening age hath wrought thee into man, the very voyager shall cease out of the sea, nor the sailing pine exchange her merchandise: all lands shall bear all things, the ground shall not suffer the mattock, nor the vine the pruning-hook; now likewise the strong ploughman shall loose his bulls from the yoke.

Trans. J. W. Mackail

8   **mortālis, mortālis,** M.: human being, mortal.
       praeter, preposition with acc.: besides, except.
       lītus, lītoris, N.: shore.
       nōrant = **nōverant,** from **nōscō, nōscere, nōvī, nōtum:** to
          learn, know.

9   **praeceps, praecipitis:** steep, precipitous.
       cingō, cingere, cīnxī, cīnctum: to gird, surround.
       fossa, fossae, F.: ditch, trench.

10   **tuba, tubae,** F.: bugle, war trumpet.
       dīrēctus, -a, -um: straight; sc. **aeris.**
       aes, aeris, N.: bronze.
       cornū, cornūs, N.: horn.
       flexus, -a, -um: curved.

11   **galea, galeae,** F.: helmet.
       ēnsis, ēnsis, M.: sword.
       mīles, mīlitis, M.: soldier, army.
       ūsus, ūsūs, M.: use, need.

12   **mollis, molle:** soft, gentle, easy.
       sēcūrus, -a, -um: carefree.
       peragō, peragere, perēgī, perāctum: to live a life of.
       ōtium, ōtiī, N.: leisure, retirement, relaxation.

13   **ipsa:** modifies **tellūs,** line 14.
       immūnis, immūne: without effort or cost.
       rāstrum, rāstrī, N.: rake, hoe.
       intāctus, -a, -um: untouched, uninjured.
       ūllus, -a, -um: any.

14   **saucius, -a, -um:** wounded, injured.
       vōmer, vōmeris, M.: plowshare.
       tellūs, tellūris, F.: the earth or, personified, Mother Earth.

15   **contentus, -a, -um:** content, satisfied (takes abl.).
       cibus, cibī, M.: food.
       nūllō cōgente: "with no compelling," i.e., with no active
          cultivation.
       creātīs: "created," "produced."

16   **arbuteus, -a, -um:** of the arbutus tree (a kind of wild straw-
          berry).
       fētus, fētūs, M.: produce, fruit.
       frāga, frāgōrum, N. pl.: wild strawberries.
       montānus, -a, -um: mountain.

cornaque et in dūrīs haerentia mōra rubētīs 17

et, quae dēciderant patulā Iovis arbore, glandēs. 18

Vēr erat aeternum, placidīque tepentibus aurīs 19

mulcēbant zephyrī nātōs sine sēmine flōrēs; 20

mox etiam frūgēs tellūs inarāta ferēbat, 21

nec renovātus ager gravidīs cānēbat aristīs: 22

flūmina iam lactis, iam flūmina nectaris ībant, 23

flāvaque dē viridī stillābant īlice mella. 24

Drawing of Ovid, from the frontispiece to the Delphin edition of the poet's works (London; Valpy, 1821).

17 **cornum, cornī, N.**: cornel cherry.
haerentia: "clinging."
mōrum, mōrī, N.: blackberry, mulberry.
rubētum, rubētī, N.: bramble thicket.

18 **dēcidō, decidere, decidī**: to fall down.
patulus, -a, -um: spreading, broad.
Iūppiter, Iovis, M.: Jupiter, sky-god and chief deity of the
   Romans.
arbor, arboris, F.: tree; sc. **dē.**
glāns, glandis, F.: nut, acorn.

19 **vēr, vēris, N.**: spring.
aeternus, -a, -um: eternal.
placidus, -a, -um: peaceful, placid.
tepēns, tepentis: warm, warming.
aura, aurae, F.: breeze.

20 **mulceō, mulcēre, mulsī, mulsum**: to stir gently, soothe.
zephyrus, zephyrī, M.: west wind.
nātōs: "sprung forth," "born."
sēmen, sēminis, N.: seed.
flōs, flōris, M.: flower.

21 **frūx, frūgis, F.**: grain.
inarātus, -a, -um: unplowed, untilled.
ferēbat: "brought forth."

22 **nec renovātus = et nōn renovātus**: "and though not plowed."
gravidus, -a, -um: loaded, filled, pregnant.
cāneō, cānēre, cānuī: to become white.
arista, aristae, F.: an ear or stalk of grain.

23 **lac, lactis, N.**: milk.
nectar, nectaris, N.: nectar (drink of the gods).
ībant: "were flowing."

24 **flāvus, -a, -um**: yellow, golden.
viridis, viride: green, verdant.
stillō, stillāre, stillāvī, stillātum: to drip.
īlex, īlicis, F.: the holm-oak.
mel, mellis, N.: honey.

Comprehension Questions

LINES 1-12

1. In the Golden Age men behaved justly of their own accord; what goads or incentives to just action were *not* present and *not* required?
2. In these first twelve lines three activities common to human society are alluded to—what are they?

LINES 13-24

1. What fourth activity common to human society is referred to in these lines?
2. How was food produced during the Golden Age? What was man's role?
3. How is the arrangement of the words in the phrase *in dūrīs haerentia mōra rubētīs* (line 17) appropriate to the meaning of the phrase?
4. What weather conditions prevailed in the Golden Age?
5. What phrase in verse 22 essentially repeats the phrase *tellūs inarāta* in verse 21?

UNIT SIX

MARTIAL'S *LIBER SPECTACULORUM:* THE GAMES IN THE COLOSSEUM

Introduction

MARTIAL'S LIFE AND WORKS

The epigrammatist Martial (Marcus Valerius Martialis), one of the most popular of Latin poets, was born at Bilbilis in Spain around A.D. 40. He moved to Rome in 64, where he appears at first to have lived in meager circumstances; gradually, however, he advanced in social status, gained appointment as an honorary military tribune, and came to know, seemingly on friendly terms, several contemporary literary figures, including Pliny the Younger, the educator Quintilian, and the satirist Juvenal.

In A.D. 80 Martial published the *Liber Spectaculorum* ("Book of the Games"), commemorating the opening by the emperor Titus of the Flavian Amphitheater, or the "Colosseum" as it came to be called after the colossal statue of Nero that towered nearby; a few years later, in 84-85, he published two more collections of chiefly two-line epigrams, the *Xenia* ("Guest Gifts") and *Apophoreta* ("Take-Home Gifts"), written to accompany presents for dinner-guests and friends. Martial is most famous, however, for his *Epigrammaton Libri,* a collection of over a thousand epigrams in twelve books published from 86 to ca. 101. In these short poems, usually no more than six to twelve lines in length and most of them in the elegiac meter, the epigrammatist vividly and succinctly depicted Roman men and women of all ages and walks of life in a humorous, often satiric (and sometimes obscene) manner. The Epigrams immediately captured public attention and became an important source for Martial's younger contemporary Juvenal; they remain popular today and provide ancient historians with valuable glimpses of Roman society in the first century after Christ.

Martial seems never to have married, but his compassionate nature can be felt in poems about children, his friends, and slaves. He retired to his native Spain in A.D. 98, at the accession of the emperor Trajan and so perhaps for political reasons (neither Trajan nor his predecessor Nerva, A.D. 96-98, would have been pleased with the unrestrained flattery the poet had heaped upon the emperor Domitian throughout his fifteen-year reign, 81-96). After publishing the twelfth book of his Epigrams from Spain in 101, Martial died, in 104, without ever returning to Rome.

THE *LIBER SPECTACULORUM* AND THE GAMES IN THE COLOSSEUM

In the thirty-three short poems of his "Book of the Games," all of them in the elegiac meter, Martial celebrates the dedication of the Colosseum by the emperor Titus (who reigned only for the brief period A.D. 79-81) and describes many of the sorts of spectacles that were produced in that arena for the public entertainment. The Colosseum, measuring over 600 feet across (188 meters) at its greatest width, over 150 feet (48.5 meters) in height, and with a capacity for some 50,000 spectators, was a monumental architectural accomplishment whose construction required several years; the entertainments provided there at state expense included a variety of gladiatorial contests, wild animal fights, and even, with the arena flooded for the purpose, mock naval battles. The five selections presented below illustrate some of these events and, in the first instance, Martial's pride in the Amphitheater itself; the meter is the elegiac couplet.

Martial *Liber Spectaculorum* 1

Barbara pȳramidum sileat mīrācula Memphis,   1

Assyrius iactet nec Babylōna labor;   2

nec Triviae templō mollēs laudentur Iōnēs;   3

dissimulet Dēlon cornibus āra frequēns;   4

āere nec vacuō pendentia Mausōlēa   5

1   **barbarus, -a, -um:** barbaric; modifies Memphis (adjective and noun were often widely separated in Latin verse: cf. **Assyrius . . . labor** in line 2).

pȳramis, pȳramidis, F.: pyramid; the Egyptian pyramids were among the "seven wonders of the ancient world."

sileat: "let (him, her, it) not tell"; here, "let Memphis not tell."

mīrāculum, mīrāculī, N.: miracle, wonder.

Memphis, Memphis, F.: Memphis, a city of Lower Egypt; here, the people of Memphis.

2   **Assyrius, -a, -um:** Assyrian; of Assyria (in Mesopotamia). **Assyrius . . . nec = nec Assyrius;** conjunctions, for metrical reasons, were often delayed in Latin poetry.

iactet: "let (him, her, it) boast of."

Babylōn, Babylōnis, F.: Babylon, a city on the Euphrates River, renowned for its architecture; the form here is a Greek accusative singular.

3   **Trivia, Triviae, F.:** Diana (the Greek Artemis), goddess of the woodlands and the hunt; her temple at Ephesus, referred to here, was another of the seven wonders.

templum, templī, N.: temple, shrine; here, abl. of cause.

mollis, mollis: soft, luxurious.

laudentur: "let (them) be praised."

Iōnēs, Iōnum, M. pl.: the inhabitants of Ionia, on the west coast of Asia Minor.

4   **dissimulet:** "let (him, her, it) keep hidden."

Dēlos, Dēlī, F.: Delos, an island in the Aegean Sea, mythical birthplace of Apollo and famous for its shrine to that god; the form here is Greek accusative.

cornibus āra frequēns: "the altar made of many horns," from animals slain by Diana, according to legend; the altar was another ancient marvel.

5   **āēr, āeris, M.:** air; sc. **in** (prepositions usual in Latin prose were often omitted in poetry).

vacuus, -a, -um: empty.

pendentia: "hanging," "hovering"; the lofty building was seemingly suspended in the air.

Mausōlēum, Mausōlēī, N.: the tomb of King Mausolus at Halicarnassus, a city of Caria in southwestern Asia Minor.

58

laudibus immodicīs Cāres in astra ferant.   6

Omnis Caesareō cēdit labor amphitheātrō;   7

ūnum prō cūnctīs fāma loquētur opus.   8

Page from a fifteenth-century Roman edition of the Liber Spectaculorum *(from G. Norcio, ed.,* Epigrammi de Marziale, *Turin: Unione Tipographico-Editrice, 1980).*

6   **laus, laudis,** F.: praise.
     immodicus, -a, -um: immodest, excessive.
     Cār, Cāris, M.: an inhabitant of Caria.
     astrum, astrī, N.: star; the sky.
     ferant: "let (them) exalt."
7   **Caesareus, -a, -um:** of Caesar, specifically here of the Fla-
          vian emperors, Vespasian, Titus, and Domitian (who
          succeeded his brother Titus in A.D. 81, a year after
          the dedication of the Colosseum).
     amphitheātrum, amphitheātrī, N.: amphitheater.
8   **cūnctus, -a, -um:** all.
     loquētur: "shall speak of."

The Flavian Amphitheatre, from the west (photo, C. Thomas Poss).

Liber Spectaculorum 6b

Prōstrātum vastā Nemeēs in valle leōnem   1

    nōbile et Herculeum fāma canēbat opus.   2

Prīsca fidēs taceat: nam post tua mūnera, Caesar,   3

    haec iam fēmineā dīcimus ācta manū.   4

1 **prōstrātum:** "slain."
   vastus, -a, -um: vast, broad.
   Nemeēs: "of Nemea," a valley in the Greek Argolid where
      Hercules performed the first of his twelve labors,
      squeezing to death a ferocious lion whose hide was
      impenetrable.
   vallēs, vallis, F.: valley.
   leō, leōnis, M.: lion.
2 **nōbile et Herculeum . . . opus:** in apposition to line 1.
   Herculeus, -a, -um: Herculean.
   canō, canere, cecinī: to sing of, celebrate, extol.
   opus, operis, N.: work, deed, labor.
3 **prīscus, -a, -um:** ancient.
   fidēs, fideī, F.: faith, belief.
   taceat: "let (him, her, it) be silent."
   mūnus, mūneris, N.: public show, gladiatorial show.
4 **fēmineus, -a, -um:** feminine, woman's.
   ācta = ācta esse, "have been accomplished."

Not all Romans were favorably impressed with the appearance of female gladiators in the arena. The satirist Juvenal (see Unit Seven and illustration, p. 80, below) complained, for example, of a woman named Mevia who participated, rather immodestly, in a wild boar hunt (*Satires* 1.23-24, 30):

Cum . . . Mevia Tuscum
figat aprum et nuda teneat venabula mamma
. . . . .
difficile est saturam non scribere.

when Mevia goes pig-sticking and carries
her spears over her naked breast . . . it's
difficult *not* to write satire!

              R.A.L.

Liber Spectaculorum 9

Praestitit exhibitus tōtā tibi, Caesar, harēnā	1
quae nōn prōmīsit proelia rhīnocerōs.	2
Ō quam terribilīs exārsit prōnus in īrās!	3
Quantus erat taurus, cui pila taurus erat!	4

The Romans were fascinated with exotic animals from the east and Africa; a rhinoceros is depicted in this detail from a Praeneste mosaic (photo, Robert I. Curtis).

1 **praestō, praestāre, praestitī, praestitum:** to provide, present.
   exhibitus, -a, -um: exhibited, on display.
   harēna, harēnae, F.: arena.
2 **prōmittō, prōmittere, prōmīsī, prōmissum:** to promise.
   proelium, proeliī, N.: fight, battle.
   rhīnocerōs, rhīnocerōtis, M.: rhinoceros.
3 **terribilis, terribile:** frightening, dreadful; the form here is
     accusative plural (= **terribilēs**).
   exārdēscō, exārdēscere, exārsī: to blaze up.
   prōnus, -a, -um: bent; here, "with head lowered."
4 **quantus, -a, -um:** how great, how large.
   taurus, taurī, M.: bull, the word refers here, in the first
     instance, to the great bull rhinoceros being exhibited
     and, in the second, to an actual bull, small by com-
     parison, which was sent into the arena to enrage the
     rhinoceros.
   pila, pilae, F.: a ball or dummy of cloth and straw thrown
     into the arena to incite the wild animals on display.

Liber Spectaculorum 17

Quod pius et supplex elephās tē, Caesar, adōrat   1

   hic modo quī taurō tam metuendus erat,   2

nōn facit hoc iussus, nūllōque docente magistrō: 3

   crēde mihī, nostrum sentit et ille deum.   4

Elephants frequently appeared on Roman coins, as on this denarius of Julius Caesar (British Museum).

1   **quod:** "as to the fact that."
       pius, -a, -um: devoted, loyal.
       supplex, supplicis: suppliant, humble.
       elephās, elephantis, M.: elephant.
       adōrō, adōrāre, adōrāvī, adōrātum: to adore, worship.
2   **modo,** adverb: just a while ago; **modo quī** = **quī modo.**
       metuendus: "to be feared," "frightening."
3   **iussus:** "having been ordered (to do so)"; modifies **elephās.**
           With **nōn,** freely, "without being ordered" or "un-
           bidden."
       docente: "teaching" or "training"; modifies **magistrō.**
       magister, magistrī, M.: master, teacher.
4   **crēdō, crēdere, crēdidī, crēditum:** to believe, trust (with
           dat.).
       nostrum . . . deum: prose word order would be **et ille deum
           nostrum sentit.**
       sentiō, sentīre, sēnsī, sēnsum: to sense, perceive.
       et = **etiam,** as often in poetry.

Bust of Titus (Capitoline Museum, Rome; photo, James C. Anderson, Jr.).

Liber Spectaculorum 24

Sī quis ades longīs sērus spectātor ab ōrīs,	1
cui lūx prīma sacrī mūneris ista fuit,	2
nē tē dēcipiat ratibus nāvālis Enȳō	3
et pār unda fretīs: hīc modo terra fuit.	4
Nōn crēdis? Spectā, dum lassant aequora Martem:	5
Párva mora est, dīcēs "Hīc modo pontus erat."	6

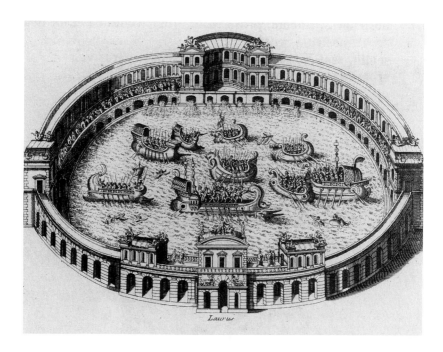

Drawing of a naumachia, *a mock naval battle, in an arena (Mansell Collection).*

1   **sī quis ades:** "whoever you are who are here."
    sērus, -a, -um: late, late-coming.
    spectātor, spectātōris, M.: spectator; predicate nominative
        after **ades.**
    ōra, ōrae, F.: coast, shore.
2   **lūx:** here = **diēs.**
    prīma: predicate adjective.
    sacer, -cra, -crum: sacred.
3   **nē . . . dēcipiat:** "let (him, her, it) not deceive."
    ratis, ratis, F.: ship, boat.
    nāvālis, nāvāle: of ships.
    Enyō, Enyūs, F.: a Greek goddess of war; here, a person-
        ification of a naval battle.
4   **pār, paris,** adjective with dat.: equal, similar, comparable
        (to).
    unda, undae, F.: wave.
    fretum, fretī, N.: strait, channel, the sea.
5   **lassō, lassāre, lassāvī, lassātum:** to tire, weary.
    aequor, aequoris, N.: the sea.
    Mars, Martis, M.: Mars, the Roman god of war.
6   **mora, morae,** F.: delay.
    pontus, pontī, M.: the sea.

Comprehension Questions

LIBER SPECTACULORUM (L.S.) 1

1. How many of the Seven Wonders of the Ancient World does Martial allude to? What are they?
2. Which nations does Martial bid to be silent?
3. Which nations or monuments are not to be praised?
4. What is *fāma* to proclaim?

L.S. 6b

1. Where, specifically, did Hercules slay the lion?
2. What will people say about such Herculean deeds, once Caesar has produced his gladiatorial shows in the Colosseum?

L.S. 9

1. What two animals were matched in this fight?
2. What did the rhinoceros do when he was enraged?

L.S. 17

1. What was the elephant's attitude toward Caesar?
2. What has not motivated the elephant's behavior?
3. What has motivated it?

L.S. 24

1. Who is the addressee of this epigram?
2. Where does he come from?
3. What is this day for him?
4. What is he not to be deceived by?
5. How do we say *parva mora est* in modern idiomatic English?

UNIT SEVEN

JUVENAL'S THIRD SATIRE: DANGERS OF THE ROMAN NIGHT

Introduction

JUVENAL'S LIFE AND WORKS

Little is known for certain of the life of Decimus Junius Juvenalis (Juvenal), the last, and one of the greatest, of Rome's satirists. Born ca. A.D. 60 in the Latin town of Aquinum, possibly the son of a well-to-do freedman, Juvenal appears to have served as a young man in the Roman army, perhaps in Britain, and then to have held public office in Aquinum. He was well educated in rhetoric and literature and soon took up a career as a rhetorician in Rome, where at least by the early 90s he became a friend of the epigrammatist Martial. There is a tradition, confused and untrustworthy in its details, that he was exiled to Egypt at some point by the emperor Domitian.

Juvenal was living at Rome, in any case, when he published the first of his five books of Satires ca. A.D. 110, under the emperor Trajan, and he seems to have remained there until his death about twenty years later during the reign of Hadrian. The sixteen Satires, which enjoyed little popularity in Juvenal's own day, doubtless in part because of their generally caustic tone and pessimistic outlook, have remained favorites of European readers from the fourth century onward; Satires Three, on the evils of life in the city of Rome, Six, on the wicked ways of women, Eight, on nobility of character as opposed to nobility of birth, and Ten, on the folly of man's usual wishes and prayers, are often included in college literature surveys.

Continuing the tradition of verse satire established by Lucilius in the late second century B.C. and refined by Horace eighty years later, but adopting the genre to his own peculiar perspective and temperament, Juvenal claimed to survey with the satirist's critical eye a broad range of human behavior. "Whatever men do," Juvenal wrote in Satire 1, "their prayers, their hopes, their fears, what angers them, gives them pleasure, delights them, all this is the mixed mash of my little book" (Satire 1. 85-86: *quidquid agunt homines, votum, timor, ira, voluptas, / gaudia, discursus, nostri farrago libelli est*); but his focus was really narrower, as he indicated in the very next verse (Satire 1.87), "And when was there ever a more abundant store of vices!" (*et quando uberior vitiorum copia*). What Juvenal actually surveys of human society is contemporary Roman society (though many of his examples, for safety's sake, are drawn from the past), the Roman upper classes for the most part, and the seamier, more vicious aspects of their behavior in particular. The Satires, all of them written in the dactylic hexameter and ranging in length from about 150 verses to the nearly 700 verses of Satire Six (Satire Sixteen, with only 60 lines, is incomplete owing to an accident of manuscript transmission), are valued by historians as sources for insights into Roman life of the second century A.D., though in that connection they must be read with an awareness of the satirist's use of exaggeration and irony. The Satires are most admired, however, for their brilliance of language, their often powerful rhetoric, epigrammatic wit, and vividness of description.

SATIRE THREE: ON THE CITY OF ROME

Juvenal's first book contained five satires, totalling something less than a thousand verses. Satire Three, the book's centerpiece, is thematically the most comprehensive poem of the volume and, with 322 lines, the longest. Following a brief introduction the poem takes the form of a diatribe against life in Rome delivered by the poet's imaginary friend Umbricius on the occasion of his departure from the city. Umbricius plans to leave Rome forever and settle at Cumae, the oldest Greek city in Italy and hence a curious choice for a fellow like Umbricius, who, with his many Archie Bunker qualities, despises all "foreigners," especially Greeks. Juvenal means us to see his "pal," an aging, unsuccessful parasite, as something of a comic malcontent; nonetheless, in the course of Umbricius' impassioned invective, the satirist permits us a glimpse at many of the ills and inconveniences of life in the imperial city.

Following his complaints against foreigners (who take all the good jobs and all the rich patrons!), the clientage system, and the misery of poverty in general (encapsulated brilliantly at 152-53, *nil habet infelix paupertas durius in se / quam quod ridiculos homines facit,* "wretched poverty has no other worse aspect than that it makes men the objects of laughter"), the disgruntled client proceeds to catalog some of the more specific evils of urban living: the overpriced, ramshackle apartment buildings (193-94: "we inhabit a city largely propped on shaky stilts"), the ever present danger of fire, the noise and the impossibility of sleep, the traffic congestion and the chance of being crushed beyond recognition by a collapsed truckload of logs or building-stone (259-60: "who will ever find your limbs, your bones?"). Concluding his account of what sound like the familiar ills of modern living in big cities even today, Umbricius turns to some of the dangers of Roman nightlife, including burglars and armed robbers (305: "one day your affairs will all be settled, in an instant, by some hoodlum with a knife") and, in the passage excerpted below (verses 268-301), bullies and—a typically Juvenalian sardonic flourish—falling rooftiles and slop-pots dropped (or thrown?) from upper-story windows that come crashing down upon your head!

Juvenal *Satires* 3.268-301

_ ⌣ / _   ⌣⌣/ _ // _/ _ ⌣ _/ _ ⌣⌣ / _ _
Respice nunc alia ac dīversa perīcula noctis: 1

_   ⌣⌣/ _ _ / _ _ / _ ⌣⌣// _ ⌣ _/ _ _
quod spatium tēctīs sublīmibus unde cerebrum   2

_ _ ⌣ /_ // ⌣ _/ _ _/ _ _ / _ _⌣⌣/ _ _
testa ferit, quotiēns rīmōsa et curta fenestrīs   3

vāsa cadant, quantō percussum pondere signent   4

et laedant silicem. Possīs ignāvus habērī   5

et subitī cāsūs imprōvidus, ad cēnam sī   6

intestātus eās: adeō tot fāta, quot illā   7

Remains (photo, Robert I. Curtis) and reconstruction (Mansell Collection) of a five-story tenement block, or insula, *at Ostia, Rome's seaport; similar* insulae *were numerous in Rome itself in the time of Juvenal.*

1   **respiciō, respicere, respexī, respectum:** to look at, take note
        of.
    dīversus, -a, -um: different, diverse.

2   **quod spatium:** sc. **sit** (= **est**).
    spatium, spatiī, N.: space, distance.
    tēctum, tēctī, N.: roof, rooftop.
    sublīmis, sublīme: high, lofty, towering.
    unde, relative adverb: from where.
    cerebrum, cerebrī, N.: brain, top of the head, skull.

3   **testa, testae,** F.: roof-tile.
    feriō, ferīre: to strike, hit, smash.
    quotiēns, interrogative adverb: how many times, how often?
    rīmōsus, -a, -um: cracked.
    curtus, -a, -um: broken.
    fenestra, fenestrae, F.: window; sc. **ex** (prepositions usual in
        prose are often omitted in verse).

4   **vāsum, vāsī,** N.: vase, jug, pot.
    cadant = cadunt, from **cadō, cadere, cecidī, cāsum,** to fall.
    quantus, -a, -um: how great? what great?
    percussum: "struck," "smashed"; modifies **silicem** (adjec-
        tive and noun were often widely separated in Latin
        poetry).
    pondus, ponderis, N.: weight.
    signent = signant, from **signō, signāre, signāvī, signātum,** to
        mark.

5   **laedant = laedunt,** from **laedō, laedere, laesī, laesum,** to
        injure, disfigure, damage.
    silex, silicis, M.: stone, pavement.
    possīs . . . habērī: "you would be considered."
    ignāvus, -a, -um: foolish, lazy.

6   **subitus, -a, -um:** sudden.
    cāsus, cāsūs, M.: accident, chance, disaster.
    imprōvidus, -a, -um: heedless, improvident.

7   **intestātus, -a, -um:** intestate, without having made a will.
    eās: "you should go."
    adeō tot . . . quot: "just as many . . . as."
    fātum, fātī, N.: fate, death, cause of death; sc. **sunt.**

nocte patent vigilēs tē praetereunte fenestrae.   8

Ergō optēs vōtumque ferās miserābile tēcum,   9

ut sint contentae patulās dēfundere pelvēs!   10

   Ēbrius ac petulāns, quī nūllum forte cecīdit,   11

dat poenās: noctem patitur lūgentis amīcum   12

Pēlīdae; cubat in faciem, mox deinde supīnus.   13

[Ergō nōn aliter poterit dormīre; quibusdam]   14

somnum rīxa facit. Sed quamvīs improbus annīs   15

Achilles binding the wounds of Patroclus; in literature, the two were symbols of profound friendship. From an Athenian red-figure cup by the Sosias painter, ca. 515 B.C. (photo, courtesy Antikenmuseum, Staatliche Museen, Berlin).

8   **pateō, patēre, patuī:** to be open, gape open.

    vigil, vigilis: awake; applied here to the windows of houses whose occupants are awake.

    tē praetereunte: "as you pass by."

9   **ergō,** adverb: therefore.

    optēs: "you should hope."

    vōtum, vōtī, N.: prayer.

    ferās: "you should carry."

    miserābilis, miserābile: wretched, pitiable.

10   **ut sint:** "that (they) may be"; sc. **fenestrae.**

    contentus, -a, -um: content, satisfied.

    patulus, -a, -um: wide-open, broad, shallow.

    dēfundō, dēfundere, dēfūdī, dēfūsum: to pour out, dump out.

    pelvis, pelvis, F.: basin, shallow bowl.

11   **ēbrius, -a, -um:** drunk, inebriated.

    petulāns, petulantis: insolent, rowdy, aggressive.

    forte, adverb: by chance, as it happened.

    caedō, caedere, cecīdī, caesum: to cut, strike, kill.

12   **dat poenās:** "pays the penalty."

    patitur: "suffers," "endures."

    lūgentis: "mourning"; modifies **Pēlīdae** (13).

13   **Pēlīdēs, Pēlīdae,** M.: the son of Peleus, Achilles; during the Trojan War Achilles long grieved over the death of his closest friend Patroclus, who had been slain by the Trojan prince Hector.

    cubō, cubāre, cubuī, cubitum: to lie down, sleep.

    faciēs faciēī, F.: face (English idiom would say, "on his stomach").

    supīnus, -a, -um: on the back, face upwards.

14   The brackets indicate that editors generally regard this line as an interpolation, i.e., a later addition, probably by some medieval scribe; one reason for this view is the illogical use of **ergō.**

    aliter, adverb: in any other way.

    quīdam, quaedam, quiddam: certain, some.

15   **somnus, somnī,** M.: sleep.

    rīxa, rīxae, F.: quarrel, brawl, fight.

    quamvīs, adverb: no matter how, even though.

    improbus, -a, -um: shameless, impudent.

atque merō fervēns cavet hunc quem coccina laena   16

vītārī iubet et comitum longissimus ōrdō,   17

multum praetereā flammārum et aenea lampas.   18

Mē, quem lūna solet dēdūcere vel breve lūmen   19

candēlae, cuius dispēnsō et tempero fīlum,   20

contemnit. Miserae cognōsce prohoemia rīxae,   21

sī rīxa est, ubi tū pulsās, ego vāpulo tantum.   22

Stat contrā stārīque iubet. Pārēre necesse est;   23

16   **merum, merī, N.:** undiluted wine.

fervēns, ferventis: hot, seething, flushed, on fire.

caveō, cavēre, cāvī, cautum: to be on guard against, keep away from.

coccinus, -a, -um: scarlet-dyed.

laena, laenae, F.: a woolen cloak or mantle.

17   **vītō, vītāre, vītāvī, vītātum:** to avoid.

comes, comitis, C.: companion, attendant.

ōrdō, ōrdinis, M.: order, rank, row, parade.

18   **multum . . . flammārum:** "many torches" (literally, "much of flames").

praetereā, adverb: besides, besides that.

aeneus, -a, -um: of bronze.

lampas, lampadis, F.: torch, lamp, lantern.

19   **lūna, lūnae, F.:** moon.

soleō, solēre, soluī, solitum: to be accustomed (to).

dēdūcō, dēdūcere, dēdūxī, dēductum: to lead down, escort.

vel, conjunction: or.

brevis, breve: brief, short, slender.

lūmen, lūminis, N.: light.

20   **candēla, candēlae, F.:** candle.

dispēnsō, dispēnsāre, dispēnsāvī, dispēnsātum: to apportion, portion out, regulate (i.e., here, to keep from burning down too quickly).

temperō, temperāre, temperāvī, temperātum: to moderate, adjust; the final, unaccented "-o" is shortened, as often in Latin verse; cf. **vāpulo** in line 22.

fīlum, fīlī, N.: thread, wick.

21   **contemnō, contemnere, contempsī, contemptum:** to despise, scorn, treat with contempt.

prohoemium, prohoemiī, N.: prologue, beginning.

22   **pulsō, pulsāre, pulsāvī, pulsātum:** to knock, beat, strike.

vāpulō, vāpulāre, vāpulāvī, vāpulātum: to be beaten, thrashed, battered.

tantum, adverb: only.

23   **contrā, adverb:** face to face, opposite (someone).

stārī: "to halt" (literally, "to be halted"); sc. **mē.**

pāreō, pārēre, pāruī, pāritum: to obey, comply, submit.

necesse, indeclinable adjective: necessary.

nam quid agās, cum tē furiōsus cōgat et īdem   24

fortior? "Unde venīs" exclāmat, "cuius acētō,   25

cuius conche tumēs? Quis tēcum sectile porrum   26

sūtor et ēlixī vervēcis labra comēdit?   27

Nīl mihi respondēs? Aut dīc aut accipe calcem!   28

Ēde ubi cōnsistās: in quā tē quaero proseuchā?"   29

Dīcere sī temptēs aliquid tacitusve recēdās,   30

tantundem est: feriunt pariter, vadimōnia deinde   31

24 **agās:** "can you do," "is one to do."

cum, conjunction: when.

furiōsus, -a, -um: mad, insane.

cōgat = **cogit.**

īdem: sc. **sit** (= **est**).

25 **exclāmō, exclāmāre, exclāmāvī, exclāmātum:** to shout, yell.

acētum, acētī, N.: sour wine, vinegar; "cheap booze."

26 **conchis, conchis,** F.: bean.

tumeō, tumēre, tumuī: to swell, bulge, be bloated (here, with the flatulence caused by beans).

quis . . . sūtor (27): "what cobbler?"

sectile porrum: "leek," "scallion."

27 **ēlixus, -a, -um:** boiled.

vervēx, vervēcis, M.: a sheep.

labrum, labrī, N.: lip.

comedō, comedere, comēdī, comēsum: to eat up, gobble.

28 **nīl** = **nihil.**

calx, calcis, F.: heel (of the foot), kick.

29 **ēdō, ēdere, ēdidī, ēditum:** to give out, tell, declare.

cōnsistō, cōnsistere, cōnstitī, cōnstitum: to stay, reside, hang out.

quaerō, quaerere, quaesīvī, quaesītum: to seek, look for (for the short "-o," see above on **tempero,** line 20).

proseucha, proseuchae, F.: synagogue.

30 **temptēs** = **temptās,** from **temptō, temptāre, temptāvī, temptātum,** to try, attempt.

aliquis, aliquid, pronoun: someone, something.

-ve, enclitic conjunction: or (**tacitusve** = **vel tacitus**).

tacitus, -a, -um: silent, quiet; here with adverbial force, "quietly."

recēdās = **recēdis,** from **recēdō, recēdere, recessī, recessum,** to retreat, move away.

31 **tantusdem, tantadem, tantundem:** much the same, all the same.

feriō, ferīre: to strike, hit, beat.

pariter, adverb: equally, just as much.

vadimōnia . . . faciunt: "they bring charges against you," "they haul you into court"; **vadimōnium** was the bond a defendant had to pay to insure his appearance in court.

īrātī faciunt. Lībertās pauperis haec est: 32

pulsātus rogat et pugnīs concīsus adōrat 33

ut liceat paucīs cum dentibus inde revertī. 34

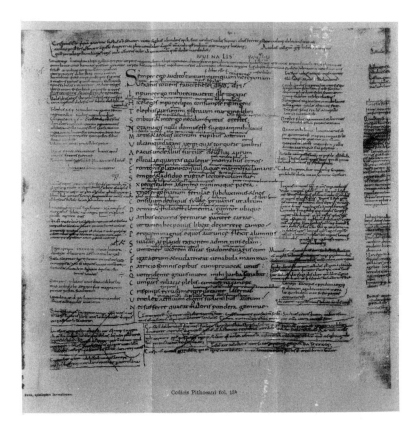

Page of the French codex Pithoeanus of Juvenal, our most important manuscript of the Satires, *dating to the ninth century; the margins are filled with explanatory notes. Lines 22-23 are transcribed above, p. 61 (photo from R. Beer,* Spicilegium Iuvenalianum, *Leipzig; 1885).*

32   **īrātus, -a, -um:** angry, enraged.
      pauper, pauperis: poor, impoverished.

33   **pulsātus . . . et concīsus:** "battered and chopped to bits."
      rogō, rogāre, rogāvī, rogātum: to ask, beg.
      pugnus, pugnī, M.: fist.
      adōrō, adōrāre, adōrāvī, adōrātum: to beg, entreat, pray.

34   **ut liceat . . . revertī:** "that he be permitted to return (home)."
      dēns, dentis, M.: tooth.
      inde, adverb: from there.

Comprehension Questions

LINES 1-10

1. To what does Juvenal direct the audience's attention in line 1?
2. What three aspects of the same peril are described in *quod spatium . . . ferit, quotiēns . . . cadant,* and *quantō . . . pondere . . . signent et laedant?*
3. How would a person be regarded who ventured out on Rome's streets at night without having first made his or her will?
4. How abundant are the opportunities for a fatal accident in the city's streets?
5. What, therefore, ought a pedestrian to pray for?

LINES 11-22

1. How does the drunken bully suffer on a night when he has not had the opportunity to kill someone?
2. What sort of potential victim does the thug avoid?
3. How does the poor man light his path at night?
4. To what does the speaker direct the audience's attention in verse 21?

LINES 23-34

1. Why must the victim submit to the bully?
2. What does the ruffian suppose the poor man has had for dinner?
3. What happens to the bully's victim, whether he tries to speak or to run away?
4. What is the most a poor man can hope for from such an encounter?

UNIT EIGHT

THOMAS OF CELANO: THE *DIES IRAE*

Introduction

THOMAS OF CELANO AND THE *DIES IRAE*

The *Dies Irae,* perhaps the best known of Latin hymns, is usually attributed to Thomas of Celano, an Italian Franciscan who lived in the first half of the thirteenth century and wrote essays on the life and miracles of St. Francis of Assisi; little else is known of his life. The highly mystical and emotional hymn tells of the "Day of Wrath," or the Judgment Day prophesied in the New Testament. On this day, according to biblical teaching, the dead of all ages will be summoned before the throne of God to be judged on the basis of their deeds in life. The *Dies Irae* is written as a prayer or meditation of a person anticipating the judgment and asking for mercy. Because of its theme, the *Dies Irae* is incorporated into the Roman Catholic *Missa pro Defunctis* (Mass for the Dead or Requiem Mass), in arrangements of the Requiem by Mozart, Verdi, and others, as well as in such musical compositions on the theme of death as Rachmaninoff's *Isle of the Dead* and Berlioz' *Symphonie Fantastique.*

MEDIEVAL LATIN VERSE

Unlike Latin poetry of the classical period, most medieval Latin poetry was written, not in quantitative meter, but in a qualitative meter based on stress accent as in English verse and with a fixed number of syllables in each line. In the *Dies Irae* this stress accent, which coincides with the natural word accent of classical Latin, is placed, in a trochaic pattern, on the first syllable of each eight-syllable line and on every second syllable following. Another departure from classical practice in medieval verse is the use of rhyme; in this hymn the last two syllables of the three lines in each stanza are rhymed (the only exception is in the last six verses, which were a later addition designed to incorporate the meditation as a sequence in the Mass).

By the thirteenth century, when the *Dies Irae* was written, Latin was no longer spoken with the same pronunciation which the Romans had employed. The following are the most important points of pronunciation to remember when reading medieval Latin aloud:

1. All vowels and diphthongs retain essentially their classical pronunciation except for the diphthongs *ae* and *oe,* which are pronounced like the long *a* in English (*īrae* = "eeray").
2. The consonants *c* and *g* are softened before the vowels *e* and *i* (*coget* = "cojet"; *crucem* = "croochem").
3. The combination *gn* is pronounced like the Spanish *ñ* (*digna* = "dinya").
4. The consonant "v" is pronounced as in English, not as a "w."

Much of the effect of the *Dies Irae* depends upon its almost hypnotic sound; you will want to practice reading it aloud several times.

Thomas of Celano, *Dies Irae*

Díēs írae, díēs ílla	1
sólvet saéclum ín favíllā,	2
téste Dávid cúm Sibýllā.	3
Quantus tremor est futūrus,	4
quandō Iūdex est ventūrus,	5
cūncta strictē discussūrus!	6
Tuba mīrum spargēns sonum	7
per sepulcra regiōnum	8
cōget omnēs ante thronum.	9

1   **diēs:** often F., as here, when denoting a specific or appointed day.

2   **solvō, solvere, solvī, solūtum:** to loosen, break up, dissolve.

       saeclum, saeclī, N.: generation, an age, the world, human life (shortened poetic form of **saeculum**).

       favilla, favillae, F.: ash.

3   **teste`. . . Sibyllā:** "with David as witness with the Sibyl." Both pagan and Hebrew sources are credited with foretelling the Day of Judgment: David was the second king of Israel; the Sibyl, a legendary Greco-Roman prophetess.

4   **quantus, -a, -um:** how great.

       tremor, tremōris, M.: quaking.

       est futūrus: "is to be."

5   **quandō,** adverb: when.

       iūdex, iūdicis, M.: judge; capitalized here with reference to an incarnation of God.

       est ventūrus: "is about to come."

6   **cūnctus, -a, -um:** all, the whole.

       strictē, adverb: severely, rigorously.

       discussūrus: "about to shatter"; modifies **Iūdex.**

7   **tuba, tubae, F.:** trumpet.

       mīrus, -a, -um: wondrous, astonishing.

       spargēns: "dispersing" or "echoing"; modifies **tuba.**

       sonus, sonī, M.: sound.

8   **sepulcrum, sepulcrī, N.:** tomb.

       regiō, regiōnis, F.: district, region.

9   **thronus, thronī, M.:** throne.

A trumpet first shall rend the skies
And all, wherever laid, must rise
And come unto the Bar in prisoner's
   guise.

                (From a 17th-century translation, perhaps by J. Austin.)

Mors stupēbit et nātūra,   10

cum resurget creātūra   11

iūdicantī respōnsūra.   12

Liber scrīptus prōferētur,   13

in quō tōtum continētur   14

unde mundus iūdicētur.   15

Iūdex ergō cum cēnsēbit,   16

quidquid latet appārēbit: 17

nīl inultum remanēbit.   18

Quid sum miser tunc dictūrus?   19

Quem patrōnum rogātūrus,   20

cum vix iūstus sit sēcūrus?   21

Rēx tremendae māiestātis,   22

quī salvandōs salvās grātīs,   23

salvā mē, fōns pietātis!   24

Detail of Death, from Michelangelo's "The Last Judgment," in the Sistine Chapel, 1536-41 (photo, Vatican Museums).

10   **stupeō, stupēre, stupuī**: to be stunned, dumbstruck.

11   **resurgō, resurgere, resurrēxī, resurrēctum**: to rise up again.
       cum, conjunction: when.
       creātūra: "all creation."

12   **iūdicantī**: "to the one judging," "to the judge."
       respōnsūra: "to answer."

13   **scrīptus**: "which is written."
       prōferētur: "shall be brought forth."

15   **unde**, adverb: from which.
       iūdicētur: "may be judged."

16   **ergō**, adverb: therefore.
       cēnseō, cēnsēre, cēnsuī, cēnsum: to give judgment.

17   **quisquis, quidquid**: whoever, whatever.
       lateō, latēre, latuī: to lie hidden.
       appāreō, appārēre, appāruī, appāritum: to become visible, appear.

18   **nīl = nihil**.
       inultus, -a, -um: unavenged.
       remaneō remanēre, remānsī, remānsum: to remain.

19   **sum dictūrus = dīcam**.

20   **patrōnus, patrōnī, M.**: defender, advocate.
       rogātūrus: sc. **sum**, "shall I call."

21   **vix**, adverb: scarcely.
       iūstus, -a, -um: just, righteous.
       sit: "is" (subjunctive of **est**).
       sēcūrus, -a, -um: free of care, fearless.

22   **tremendus, -a, -um**: fearful, dreadful.
       māiestās, māiestātis, F.: grandeur, majesty.

23   **salvandōs**: "those who should be saved."
       salvō, salvāre, salvāvī, salvātum: to save, redeem.
       grātīs: "freely."

24   **fōns, fontis, M.**: spring, fountain.
       pietās, pietātis, F.: devotion, benevolence.

Recordāre, Iesu pie,   25

quod sum causa tuae viae: 26

nē mē perdās illā diē!   27

Quaerēns mē, sēdistī lassus;   28

redēmistī, crucem passus: 29

tantus labor nōn sit cassus!   30

Iūste Iūdex ultiōnis,   31

dōnum fac remissiōnis   32

ante diem ratiōnis.   33

Ingemiscō tamquam reus;   34

culpā rubet vultus meus: 35

supplicantī parce, Deus!   36

Quī Marīam absolvistī   37

et latrōnem exaudīstī,   38

mihi quoque spem dedistī.   39

14   *The great day of the Lord is near,*
         near and hastening fast;
      the sound of the day of the Lord is
         bitter,
      the mighty man cries aloud there.
15   *A day of wrath is that day,*
         a day of distress and anguish,
      a day of ruin and devastation,
         a day of darkness and gloom,
      a day of clouds and thick darkness,
16   *a day of trumpet blast and battle*
         cry   (Zephaniah 1.14-16, a
      against the fortified cities   major source for the
         and against the lofty battlements.   *Dies Irae*.)

25   **recordāre:** imperative form, "remember."

       Iesu: vocative form of **Iesus,** Jesus.

       pie: vocative form of **pius, -a, -um,** kind, good.

26   **quod,** conjunction: that (the word has this meaning in medieval Latin only).

       causa, causae, F.: cause, reason.

27   **nē . . . perdās:** "do not forsake."

28   **quaerēns:** "seeking"; modifies "you," the understood subject of **sēdistī.**

       lassus, -a, -um: weary, tired.

29   **redīmō, redīmere, redēmī, redēmptum:** to buy back, ransom, redeem.

       crux, crucis, F.: cross.

       passus: "having suffered."

30   **tantus, -a, -um:** so great, such great.

       nōn sit: "may (it) not be."

       cassus, -a, -um: empty, worthless, in vain.

31   **ultiō, ultiōnis,** F.: punishment, vengeance.

32   **remissiō, remissiōnis,** F.: forgiveness, redemption.

33   **ratiō, ratiōnis,** F.: reason, account, reckoning.

34   **ingemiscō, ingemiscere, ingemuī:** to groan, moan.

       tamquam, conjunction: as, just as.

       reus, reī, M.: defendant.

35   **culpa, culpae,** F.: fault, guilt, sin.

       rubeō, rubēre: to be red, to blush.

       vultus, vultūs, M.: expression, face.

36   **supplicantī:** "one pleading," "(this) suppliant" (dat.).

       parcō, parcere, pepercī, parsum: to spare (takes dat.).

37   **Marīa, Marīae,** F.: Mary Magdalene.

       absolvō, absolvere, absolvī, absolūtum: to loosen, acquit, absolve.

38   **latrō, latrōnis,** M.: robber. The reference is to the thief whom Christ pardoned as they were both being crucified.

       exaudiō, exaudīre, exaudīvī, exaudītum: to listen to, hear favorably; **audīstī** = **audīvistī.**

Precēs meae nōn sunt dignae: 40

sed tū bonus fac benignē,   41

nē perennī cremer igne.   42

Inter ovēs locum praestā   43

et ab haedīs mē sequestrā,   44

statuēns in parte dextrā.   45

Confūtātīs maledictīs,   46

flammīs ācribus addictīs,   47

vocā mē cum benedictīs.   48

Ōrō supplex et acclīnis;   49

cor contrītum quasi cinis: 50

gere cūram meī fīnis!   51

Lacrimōsa diēs illa,   52

quā resurget ex favillā   53

iūdicandus homō reus: 54

huic ergō parce, Deus.   55

Pie Iesu Domine,   56

donā eīs requiem. Amen.   57

40　**prex, precis, F.**: request, prayer.
　　dignus, -a, -um: worthy.
41　**bonus = bone.**
　　benignē, adverb: kindly, benevolently.
42　**ne . . . cremer:** "lest I be consumed."
　　perennis, perenne: lasting, eternal.
43　**ovis, ovis, F.:** sheep.
　　praestō, praestāre, praestitī: to provide, offer.
44　**haedus, haedī, M.:** goat.
　　sequestrō, sequestrāre, sequestrāvī, sequestrātum: to keep
　　　　apart.
45　**statuēns:** "setting (me)."
　　dexter, -tra, -trum: right, right-hand.
46　**confūtātīs maledictīs . . . addictīs** (47): "when the wicked
　　　　have been silenced . . . (and) consigned."
47　**flamma, flammae, F.:** flame.
48　**benedictus, -a, -um:** blessed.
49　**ōrō, ōrāre, ōrāvī, ōrātum:** to beg, ask.
　　supplex, supplicis: kneeling, entreating, suppliant.
　　acclīnis, acclīne: bowed down.
50　**cor, cordis, N.:** heart; sc. **est.**
　　contrītum: "worn down."
　　quasi, conjunction: as, just as, like.
　　cinis, cineris, M.: ash.
52　**lacrimōsus, -a, -um:** tearful, mournful; sc. **erit.**
54　**iūdicandus:** "to be judged (as)."
　　reus, reī, M.: defendant.
55　**huic:** pronounce as a disyllable.
57　**donō, donāre, donāvī, donātum:** to give.
　　requiem = requiētem, from **requiēs, requiētis, F.:** rest, re-
　　　　spite.

Comprehension Questions

LINES 1-15

1. What will happen to the world on the Day of Wrath?
2. What two figures are mentioned as witnesses to this event?
3. What signal will call forth the dead?
4. How will the rest of nature react to this?
5. To whom will the dead answer?
6. By what means will they be judged?

LINES 16-30

1. Will the Judge know about everything that relates to his decisions?
2. Why does the speaker express apprehension in lines 19-21?
3. Whom does he call upon to save him?
4. What does he ask Christ to remember?
5. What does the speaker say of Christ's suffering on the cross?

LINES 31-45

1. What does the speaker request as a gift?
2. When does he want it?
3. To what does the speaker compare himself?
4. What is the source of his distress?
5. Two figures from the past are mentioned because they were redeemed by Christ. Who are they?
6. What specific punishment does the speaker want to avoid?
7. The righteous and the wicked are each likened to an animal. What are the animals?

LINES 46-57

1. What will be the fate of the wicked?
2. What does the speaker request for himself once this fate has been accomplished?
3. To what does he compare his heart?
4. What is his request for man the defendant?
5. What does the speaker request be given to the dead?

The Cumaean Sibyl, from Michelangelo's painting on the ceiling of the Sistine Chapel (1508-10); while churchmen were little bothered by Michelangelo's depiction of the pagan prophetess, some early theologians were disturbed at her appearance along with David in the opening stanza of the Dies Irae *(photo, Vatican Museums).*